ECO-CHIC HOME

RETHINK, REUSE & REMAKE YOUR WAY TO SUSTAINABLE STYLE

ECO-CHIC HOME

EMILY ANDERSON

Photography by Seth & Kendra Smoot

SKIPSTONE

To David, Sydney, and Sam. You make everything possible.

Published by Skipstone, an imprint of The Mountaineers Books
Printed in China

First printing 2010
13 12 11 10   5 4 3 2 1

Copy Editors: Kathleen Cubley, Kim Runciman
Design: Heidi Smets
Cover photograph: Seth and Kendra Smoot

ISBN (paperback) 978-1-59485-140-7
ISBN (ebook) 978-1-59485-402-6

Library of Congress Cataloging-in-Publication Data
Anderson, Emily, 1970-
  Eco-chic home : remake, reuse & recycle your way to sustainable style / Emily Anderson ; styling by Kendra Smoot ; photography by Seth Smoot.
      p. cm.
  Includes bibliographical references and index.
  ISBN 978-1-59485-140-7 (alk. paper)
1. Handicraft. 2. Salvage (Waste, etc.) 3. Sustainable living. I. Title.
  TT157.A5544 2010
  745.5—dc22
                              2009037025

Skipstone books may be purchased for corporate, educational, or other promotional sales. For special discounts and information, contact our Sales Department at 800-553-4453 or mbooks@mountaineersbooks.org.

Skipstone
1001 SW Klickitat Way, Suite 201
Seattle, Washington 98134
206.223.6303
www.skipstonebooks.org
www.mountaineersbooks.org

LIVE LIFE. MAKE RIPPLES.

CONTENTS

INTRODUCTION

Eco-Chic Home is about celebrating our connection to all living things, no matter how great or how small. Many of us aren't always mindful of this connection and the global impact of our individual actions. We all want a cleaner, more peaceful world. What stops us from taking steps to ensure this? While it can be difficult to comprehend just how powerful individual actions really are, even our smallest choices, when put together, truly can move mountains.

For me, these choices boil down to mindfulness, intention, and action. To live every moment understanding that you are a force in the world is what being *mindful* is all about. You can make things happen even with the smallest choice, like deciding to put that bottle in the recycling instead of in the trash. *Intention* is how you deal with mindfulness. It's what you do to make an impact. You can set your own individual intentions and make every effort to follow through. Taking *action* is how to make your intentions happen. Actions can be large or small—they might have an effect today, tomorrow, or next year.

The intention of Eco-Chic Home *is greener living*. The ideas are meant to inspire actions that will benefit you and the world. This book will show you how easy it can be to create a beautiful life and a beautiful world. Beautiful is a key element in this equation. I don't believe you need to sacrifice good design for the sake of the environment. With this in mind, my goal is to use good design to inspire you to take action.

Design, by definition, is how people relate to materials, both natural and man-made. Design is important in promoting green changes and is inextricably linked to environmentalism itself. It is integral to how we interact with materials, and how we use materials has a direct impact on the environment. Materials show up in our homes as cutlery, cookware, alarm clocks, bedding, and a myriad of other items. How we use materials has an immeasurable global impact, whether they are created from a natural resource or are man-made. The way a material is cultivated, produced, used, and ultimately disposed of is of great importance as we try to create a sustainable life. Designing ways to use and reuse materials in an environmentally friendly way is the overarching theme of this book. Hopefully, *Eco-Chic Home* will help you take action to make your life and your world a little better—one project at a time.

SUSTAINABLE STYLE
Rethinking Your World

Eco-Chic Home shows you how easy and fun it is to be sustainable. Every part of this book is about making your life easier, saving you money, and giving you more time to enjoy the good things and good people in your life. The idea in every project is to rethink how we relate to materials such as plastic bottles, old newspaper, stained clothes, and other items that are generally considered disposable.

Before we lived in a disposable world, repurposing was a way of life. The introduction of cheap materials—mainly plastic—in the fifties and sixties changed our view of the world. Overconsumption became the norm, because with cheap materials we could afford to buy what we wanted, whether or not we needed it. What we realize now is that although we might not pay at the register, those cheap goods will cost us later. For example, the massive amount of petroleum-based products we consume translates into an overdependance on oil in general, which of course is a huge geopolitical and environmental problem. There are other impacts, some of which affect you on a very personal level: your health, your bank account, your family relationships. Adopting the mantra of "rethink, reduce, and repurpose" is the beginning of making a change.

Rethinking your relationship to material goods means reconsidering the value of items you would normally throw away. Look at things for the potential of the material: Something as simple as an egg carton can add style to a string of lights, a plastic bottle can become a container, and newspaper can help you decorate for the holidays. The next important thing to do is **reducing** consumption. Try asking yourself three important questions when you buy something new: Where did it come from? What is it made of? Where will it end up when I'm done with it? That last question leads us to the idea of **repurposing** items, because we can greatly reduce our consumption simply by extending the life cycle of the things we already have. Throughout *Eco-Chic Home*, you will find inspiration and how-tos that will make rethinking, reducing, and repurposing as easy as turning the page. Each project takes an everyday item and shows you how to redesign it into something brand new (new to you, anyway!).

RETHINK

To imagine new items, first look at things such as plastic containers, cardboard boxes, and day-old newspapers as more than just trash. Each material has an intrinsic value, and with some creative thinking, you can manipulate these materials into something new. *Eco-Chic Home* includes projects for a variety of materials, both natural and man-made.

WOOD AND PAPER

Wood has many eco-issues including deforestation, cost of fuel, carbon emissions from production and transportation, and overuse of paper products derived from wood. Traditionally, most affordable furnishings were made from wood, with marble and other more expensive materials used less frequently. Most affordable furniture today is actually a composite of wood and other materials with a laminate surface that's cheaper in price and in design. Environmentally friendlier options are available, but for many people these options are too expensive. Consumers have become accustomed to inexpensive furniture and have thus lost a sense of the value of wood. However, purchasing preowned solid wood furniture is one of the smartest decisions you can make, both economically and environmentally. Wood alternatives such as cork and bamboo can be much more environmentally friendly too. Paper is derived from wood, and a great deal of deforestation is the direct result of our demand for paper products, whose production creates another impact on the environment.

METAL

Iron and aluminum are the most frequently used metals today. Both come from the earth's crust and are generally considered plentiful resources. Metal is also a commodity, bought and sold in the global marketplace. In the home, metal is most often seen as a conductor of heat and electricity. Furnaces, water heaters, air conditioners, ducts, and so on, are made of metal because it can stand up to extreme temperatures. Metal is usually very recyclable, especially because of its marketplace value. Recycling businesses have a big incentive to collect and recycle metal—mostly in the form of aluminum cans. Because metal is heavy and relatively expensive, the design applications in the home have diminished over the years in favor of lighter, cheaper materials such as plastic. Although metal can be, and often is, recycled, the environmental impact of its production is substantial. Mining for ore and then smelting it (extracting the metal) produces large amounts of waste and causes environmental degradation through emissions and soil and water contamination.

GLASS

Technically, glass is a man-made material. Glass was discovered in the earliest years of the Roman Empire; interestingly, the applications even then were in common household items such as vessels and tiles, and later windows. Today we use glass in many of the same ways, but production on a large scale is very different from the early days of glass blowing. Today, glass manufacturing happens in factories and in laboratories. The really great thing about glass is that, unlike paper, plastic, wood, and fabric, it can be recycled indefinitely—which means it will never break down, no matter how many times it is recycled. Use of glass has other eco-benefits, such as in low-emissivity windows for the home. Low-E windows, as they're usually called, control heat transfer through glass with insulated glazing. As a result, a home with low-E windows will stay cooler in the summer and warmer in the winter. Glass is the primary component in how solar panels function, as well. It covers cells that absorb heat from the sun, allowing that energy to be transferred for use in the home. We won't be making solar panels in *Eco-Chic Home*, but I hope this gives you a better understanding of just how valuable glass can be.

FABRIC

Textile manufacturing has one of the biggest impacts on our environment. Chemicals are habitually used for finishings such as "wrinkle-free," "stain-resistant," and "flame-retardant." Even if a fabric is labeled "natural," it could still be hazardous to your health. Be aware of different fabric types and the eco-impacts they have on you and on the earth. Keep an eye out for the WRAP (Worldwide Responsible Accredited Production) certification (www.wrapapparel.org). WRAP is a certification program for textile manufacturers who follow a specific set of environmental guidelines. And don't

be misled just because you see an "organic" label: This just means that the cotton, wool, silk, or other non-man-made fabric was grown without using hazardous fertilizers or pesticides. But it does not mean that chemicals and other toxins weren't used at some later point in the manufacturing process. For example, manufacturers may coat fabrics with different chemical compounds. A fabric might be treated with a hydrophilic chemical to help wick moisture away from the skin. There are eco-friendly developments emerging from chemists' laboratories, too, such as Eco-Pile, or E.C.O. Fleece, a fabric made entirely from recycled plastic bottles.

Other eco-alternatives:

Linen is made from the flax plant. Growing flax has a lower eco-impact than cotton because flax needs less water and fewer pesticides to thrive.

Hemp is a good alternative because it requires very little water and is naturally resistant to pests.

Bamboo is one of the fastest-growing crops on the planet. Bamboo is extremely hardy, requiring little or no water and pesticides to grow. However, increased demand for bamboo has resulted in some negative eco-effects; clear-cutting forests to make room for more bamboo crops is on the rise in some parts of the world.

Recycled and repurposed fabric is a rising star in everything from remade fashions to denim home insulation. *Eco-Chic Home* will show you how easy it is to repurpose used clothes in many ways.

PLASTIC

To borrow a line from the movie *The Graduate*, "I have one word for you: plastics." A man-made material engineered in the labs of companies such as Wyeth and DuPont, plastic is a huge environmental problem. But plastic is also a very important material in pretty much every aspect of modern living.

We can point the finger at plastic when trying to find something obvious to blame for today's overconsumptive society.

Plastic in its many different forms has been around since the late 1800s, but after World War II, the new plastics developed during the war exploded into the consumer marketplace. Pretty soon, houses across the country filled up with plastic accessories, from the kitchen to the bedroom. Tupperware was one of the most successful stories of this era, created by Earl Tupper and marketed through a workforce made up almost entirely of housewives. Tupperware parties became a mainstay of the suburban lifestyle, and the resealable plastic pieces greatly reduced the amount of food that spoiled. Other products were created with plastic components that were affordable because plastic was a cheap material. Formica replaced traditional wood as a popular building material, and people could now afford to buy more.

We now know that many of the chemicals used to make plastic can be toxic to humans and other living things. And plastic doesn't biodegrade, so unless it's recycled (and it isn't always, because recycling can be too costly), it will sit, and sit, and sit forever. On the other hand, without plastic, we wouldn't have many of the wonderful things that make life better— medical technology, computers, safe food storage.

Bio-based plastic alternatives are being developed at a rapid clip; you can now find biodegradable plastic items derived from corn and bamboo, for example. Some of these plastic alternatives have proven suitable for many different applications. Even with these alternatives, plastic is here to stay. And that's okay, as long as we reduce our consumption of it and recycle what we do use. Pay attention to the numbers on the bottom of plastic containers—this is how you will know what can be recycled in your area. Every recycling program is unique, but here is some general information that may help.

1–Polyethylene terephthalate (PETE): Used in drink bottles, medicine containers, ink cartridges, textiles, film, moldings. This plastic has a porous surface that can collect bacteria, so these are not ideal for reuse. Very recyclable.

2–High-density polyethylene (HDPE): Used in detergent bottles, milk containers, motor oil bottles, children's toys, bulletproof vests, shampoo and conditioner bottles. Not associated with leeching chemicals upon use. Recyclable.

3–Polyvinyl chloride (PVC): Used in shrink wrap, car dashboards, pipes, shower curtains, baby-bottle nipples. Although it is a very tough plastic, it's considered unsafe to use in food preparation when heating is involved. This plastic is rarely accepted by recycling programs.

4–Low-density polyethylene (LDPE): Used in grocery bags, food storage bags. This plastic is considered food-safe, but is not often accepted by community recycling programs.

5–Polypropylene (PP): Used in food storage containers, diapers, outdoor carpet, syrup bottles, yogurt containers. Not always recyclable.

6–Polystyrene (PS): Used in plastic cutlery, packing peanuts, Styrofoam insulation, Styrofoam food containers, hubcaps. This is a problem plastic. Research has shown that toxins may leech from this type of plastic, making it potentially hazardous. It is difficult to recycle, so it is rarely accepted by local recycling programs.

7–Other: Products in this category are a combination of any other plastics from 1–6. This is the riskiest category of plastic, because you really don't know what's in it. This is also where bisphenol A (BPA) shows up, which is now considered to be unsafe for use with food and in children's toys. This is also very difficult to recycle, and most programs will not accept it.

REDUCE

Understanding some of the issues involved with today's popular materials should kick-start your efforts to reduce your consumption. Reducing consumption isn't just good for the environment—it's good for your bank account and your psyche. Spend a day cleaning out your closets and you probably will agree. The projects in this book are meant to inspire you to consume less. Once you get into it, you'll see how much fun it is to take something you already have and transform it into something you really love. Even if you never buy a single eco-friendly product in your life, buying less stuff in general means you are making one of the greenest choices possible.

You might have noticed that over the last few years, mainstream culture has had unprecedented access to eco-products and ideas. *Eco-Chic Home* isn't about using green materials, recycling, or even reducing your carbon footprint: It's about the most significant changes we can make to improve our quality of life—consuming less, spending less money, buying fewer things, eating locally grown food, taking fewer airplane trips, and on and on. My favorite green action happens to be shopping *for used items*. The fact is, the most fabulous little things are often someone else's cast-offs. The designers and stylists I work with know this; in fact, all you have to do is open up a magazine to see the random assortment used to create a lovely layout. And the best way to find your own beautiful things is to shop where the pros shop—flea markets, thrift stores, and estate sales. I think you'll also find this to be the most marvelous way to go green.

FLEA MARKETS

You might be surprised to know that the origin of the term "flea market" may have nothing to do with finding those little bugs in the items for sale. One story is that Marie Antoinette, while gazing down upon a Paris market from the castle high above it, remarked how all the people looked like little fleas. The Paris Flea Market is also said to be the first one, started by industrious individuals reclaiming cast-offs from the upper class. From the beginning, flea markets have been a unique experience. What makes them so different are the people who make a living selling their wares. The flea market community is almost like a subculture unto itself; many vendors work at the same market for decades. As a flea market shopper, you have the distinct opportunity to step inside someone else's world. Most often, the vendors sell things they themselves enjoy and collect. I like knowing that the items have been lovingly collected, however old they may be.

THRIFT STORES

Thrift stores are a mainstay for the eco-chic shopper. I like to frequent stores that support a charity effort, such as one of my favorites, Housing Works (www.housingworks.com) in New York City. Find out when new merchandise is put on the floor or when things get marked down even more. Thrift stores are a great place to stock up on wool sweaters that you can turn into felt (you'll see some of the imaginative ways you can use felt to spruce up your home later in the book). You can also find many cool fabric choices in the form of clothing, such as a shirt that you might not be caught dead in but that just might make a fabulous throw pillow. Thrift stores are the perfect place to hone your eco-chic approach to materials and how they can be repurposed.

ESTATE SALES

Estate sales are a great opportunity to pick up some real finds, because they're basically a complete household that's for sale. The difference between an estate sale and a yard sale is that you will literally be going through someone's house room by room. Chances are that very little has been done to prepare items, so imagine if you went to your friend's house and opened doors and closets—that's what this experience will be like. Be prepared to enter another person's world.

STYLE FILE: FAMOUS FLEAS

The Paris Flea Market
Paris, France

The history of the flea market goes back several centuries. In 1841, King Louis Philippe had a twenty-four-mile-long wall with a total of fifty-two gates built around Paris. The huge iron gates closed at nightfall. The other side of the large walls that surrounded the king's castle is where the first rag-and-bone men set up after 1860. These men traveled through the city by night, searching for old objects that had been thrown out with the rubbish, which they would then resell at the local markets. Between 1880 and 1900, a visitor who left Paris via the Porte de Clignancourt would travel past the hovels of the rag-and-bone men and the makeshift market stalls and inns set up in the middle of the fields and market gardens. It was here, along the passageway that separated Paris from the town of Saint-Ouen, that what became known as the Paris Flea Market began. These days the Paris Flea Market has trans-formed into something of a tourist destination, with much higher-priced goods than when the rag-and-bone men used to hawk their wares, but it still has treasures to be found (source: Les Puces de Paris Saint-Ouen, www.parispuces.com).

The Antiques Garage
New York City

The Antiques Garage is so named because it takes place in a parking garage in New York City on West 25th Street in Chelsea. Sheltered inside, rain or shine, you are sure to find antiques, vintage collectibles, furniture, clothing, shoes, and so on. You'll discover lots of odd and interesting things you didn't think you needed until you happen upon them here in this wonderful labyrinth of ephemera.

The Brooklyn Flea
Brooklyn, New York

A baby in the world of flea markets, the Brooklyn Flea has become as popular as living in Brooklyn has during the last ten years. Although it began just a few years ago, it's already expanded and moved to a bigger location. I love the way the Brooklyn Flea markets itself, and it has a really cool thing called the Hunt. Once a week it posts several random items on its website, and hosts what is basically a scavenger hunt. The items are hidden with different vendors, and the flea attendees who choose to play must find one of the items: If you do, that item is yours for free. Fun, right?

The Brimfield Antiques Show
Brimfield, Massachusetts

The Brimfield Antiques Show, commonly known as the Brimfield Flea Market, started in 1959. Brimfield is considered the largest outdoor antique show in the country. The show runs Tuesday through Sunday three times a year in May, July, and September. There are approximately five thousand dealers in twenty-one different show venues (often referred to as fields). The show covers one mile. During the flea market, Brimfield's population of 3,000 hosts more than 30,000 visitors.

Covent Garden Market and
Portobello Market
London, England

Covent Garden Market is the largest market in England, operating Monday to Saturday from 10 AM to 6 PM. Many of the items are what the English call "collectible nostalgia": a wide array of glassware and ceramics, leather goods, toys, clothes, hats, and jewelry. Covent Garden Market also features a wide selection of handmade items, often sold directly by the craftspeople. Over the past four decades, the Portobello Market has become synonymous with antiques. It's primarily a Saturday happening, from 6 AM to 5 PM. Once known mainly for fruit and vegetables (still sold throughout the week), Portobello now hosts many antique sellers, not all of whom are reputable. Word of mouth is the best way to determine which vendors you should patronize. You'll also just have to trust your instincts, which hopefully you will perfect by hitting some local fleas before you cross the pond!

GARAGE AND YARD SALES

These can sometimes be a treasure trove, but you have to get there early before everything gets picked over. Explore other communities beyond your own neighborhood. When you travel to other states, why not hit some yard sales while you're there? But keep in mind that a yard sale is someone else's chance to unload stuff they no longer want—so don't go crazy and end up with a bunch of junk destined for your next yard sale. Also remember that all prices are negotiable, you should have lots of single dollar bills on hand, and don't ever leave something with the intention of coming back for it later—chances are a bigger offer will come along and you'll be left empty-handed.

LIBRARIES AND SCHOOLS

Old books are extremely useful for a multitude of creative projects. Old pages from books work nicely in collage, decoupage, and papier-mâché projects. The hard covers are also good materials for making handmade journals, photo frames, or other creative projects. Libraries and schools will sometimes host sales where you can snatch up some books for projects. Schools may also have sales with furniture that you can repurpose.

THE INTERNET

Collectors.com is the place to go to find flea markets anywhere in the country. Etsy.com is an indispensable resource for the non-big-box store person. Full of handmade goodies, supplies, fabric, ideas, and ephemera, you can find pretty much anything you are looking for to help with your crafty endeavors. Freecycle.org lists networks of local users looking to find something used or give away their items. Craigslist and eBay sell anything and everything.

FRIENDS AND FAMILY

Don't discount the possibility that cool used items may be only a phone call away. Just because your friends and neighbors don't want something doesn't mean it isn't exactly what you're looking for. I especially love trading clothes with my sisters. Who doesn't appreciate a good hand-me-down? Thanks to the generosity of my grandparents I have many lovely, quality items to enjoy in my home for years to come. I think some of the best things to pass along are kids' toys, and I always keep the next person in mind when I encourage my kids to take good care of things. That means keeping sticky fingers clean and learning to put all the pieces away!

SWAP MEETS

At a true swap meet, no money exchanges hands. Otherwise, what you're really talking about is a flea market, where you pay for other people's items. I've found the most effective swap meets are often online. The Freecycle Network (www.freecycle.org) is dedicated to bringing people together at the local level to find and give away items for free. It's all about reuse and keeping items out of landfills. Another place to find fellow swappers is on community portals like Craigslist (www.craigslist.org). You may be lucky enough to live in an area where some crafty individuals plan live swap meets. Often these are for specific items, such as sewing and crafting supplies or handmade goods.

SALVAGE STORES

A wonderful result of the growing green market is the appearance of businesses that are built exclusively on salvaging materials from construction sites. Salvage companies operate like any other retail business, and more and more of these companies are opening, which makes this a viable option for finding great used furniture and fixtures for your home. If you're shopping for kitchen cabinets or doors, the quality of wood you'll find will certainly be higher than if you got the same thing in precut plywood from the hardware store. (For specific salvage companies, see the Eco-Chic Home Resource Guide at the end of the book.)

TEN WAYS TO REDUCE

1. Organize your home.

This book is all about coming to terms with your stuff and helping you slow down the process of accumulation. Living sustainably takes a little strategic planning on your part, which you can do only if you know where everything in your house is.

Give your household an audit by going room to room and creating a list of everything you own. Most of us are totally out of touch with how much stuff we really have. Once you have an idea of what's there, designate a space as a holding room. Put three bins in the room (large trash cans work well), label one "Donate," one "Repurpose," and one "Needs Repairs." Throughout the year, organize items in the appropriate bins. There are multiple ways to get rid of things and none of them include a landfill. You can donate items, sell items at swap meets, or trade items for things you do want. Electronic and computer companies like Dell and Apple have sophisticated programs to reuse equipment. You can sell items online via eBay or Craigslist. Freecycle is another excellent way to get rid of things that may no longer serve a purpose in your life but might be just what someone else is looking for. Give the rest to a local charity. If you're not ready to get rid of something but have no real use for it, maybe it can be remade to serve a purpose in your home.

2. Rethink trash.

A lot of the packaging that comes into your house can be put to good use. Take the time to think about that empty container before throwing it in the trash or the recycling bin. All it takes is an open mind and a little imagination.

Keeping packaging is a good way to remind ourselves of how much we actually consume, and it can serve as an everyday incentive to think before we accumulate more items. The packaging of many products is as much as 40 percent of the total cost to produce that item (source: Consumer Packaged Goods industry). Basics such as cardboard, newspaper, magazines, plastic bottles, aluminum, foil, and glass jars are all valuable resources, and although some of these materials can be recycled, the more we can reuse in our own homes, the less impact we will have on our environment.

SHOPPING TIPS

Shopping secondhand takes patience and perseverance. It also takes a fine editing skill that you can develop over time if you don't already have it. Sometimes a shopping trip is just for finding inspiration and no purchase is necessary. You may enjoy a good flea market, or maybe you prefer estate sales. Some people are avid yard sale shoppers, but you might just like to sit at your computer looking for a bargain. Whatever you prefer, start honing your hunting skills and you'll quickly learn what does and doesn't work for you.

1. To find sales in your area, check the classifieds, local community boards, and community websites.
2. Keep your eyes open for signs posted around your neighborhood; often people will put up these announcements in advance of the sale date.
3. Always bring your own shopping bags and some water, and wear comfortable shoes.
4. A GPS is a great investment for the serious yard sale shopper.
5. Don't show up earlier than the designated time. I can remember having yard sales where people would show up the day before! So annoying, and definitely not a good way to ingratiate yourself to the seller with whom you will (possibly) be negotiating prices. Some people even believe in showing up later, their theory being that the seller is more willing to negotiate prices a few hours in.
6. Don't be afraid to bargain— remember that prices are never set in stone. It's a good idea to get the seller to set the price first and then negotiate from there.
7. Bring cash, with lots of small bills. If you negotiate a price down to something like $1 from $1.50, then pay with a $20 bill, it could be awkward.
8. Look at things for their potential use: What would a coat of paint or some new fabric do? Many a quality item is hidden under years of neglect and dust.

9. When buying dishes or glass-ware, run your fingers over the surface to be sure there are no nicks or chips.

10. Don't be afraid to walk away (or click away) without buying something. Sometimes I feel guilty walking out of a store if I don't make a purchase (why, I don't know), and when it's some-one's personal stuff, the guilt factor can be even higher. But don't give in to the guilt; only purchase things you really want, otherwise you'll be setting them out in your own yard sale some-day soon.

3. Start a collection.

You may already have a collection (or collections) and not even know it. Take an inventory of your stuff to see if you do. Otherwise, pick something you like and start collecting it. I know the theme of this book is less accumula-tion, not more, but there is a method to my madness: By focusing on a key item, such as milk glass, you give your-self permission to buy pretty things, but in a concentrated and controlled way. Plus, collections can be displayed to great effect, and they can also be useful. This is also a way to exert more discipline in your shopping behavior because you are spending money on treasures rather than on whims that randomly catch your fancy. Developing a collection of useful household items is an especially practical way to fulfill your urge to shop, as well as to help you build something that can be a valuable part of your household. I collect serving trays; maybe you prefer Depression-era glass. Find a space in your home to display your collection, one that you can access when you want to use the pieces.

4. Be your own interior decorator.

You may be an accountant or a chef. Whatever your real job is, consider yourself your own personal interior decorator, too. Nobody knows your style or what makes you happy better than you do. Think of home decorating in the same way you think of getting dressed—how your home looks affects how you feel as much as what you wear does. Wearing flattering clothes is the same thing as decorating your home with appealing things. Take a page from the professional decorators and create your own personal color palette. Get a color wheel at your local art store and use it to guide you as you organize your home and make design decisions—it's amazing what using complementary colors can do in your home. Create an idea board or an idea box for inspiration. Fill it with things you find in magazines and other sources.

5. Learn something new.

Creating is a natural human instinct. Take some classes and learn to sew, knit, or cook. Making your own stuff saves money and resources and can be very fulfilling. In the long run, you'll save time, too. Research shows that people who are lifelong learners have longer, healthier, happier lives.

6. Take care of your things.

You probably heard that a lot when you were growing up. Take your shoes off when you come inside, check. Keep your good clothes and your play clothes separate, check. Sit at the table when you eat, keep all four chair legs on the floor, use wooden spoons with nonstick pans—check, check, check. These simple rules will help keep your things nicer and longer, save you money, and keep more items out of the waste stream. When things last longer, you can be more discriminating about what you buy.

7. Buy less, spend more.

We've been trained to save money and buy more. But I challenge you to buy things that are of higher quality and skip the cheap, disposable stuff—

you will save money in the long run. Only buy what you love or absolutely need. As legendary designer William Morris once said, "Have nothing in your house that you do not know to be useful or believe to be beautiful." Avoid impulse buying—waiting a few days or even a few weeks doesn't mean you will miss your window of opportunity. Be discriminating. For example, quality sheets can be very expensive, but there's a good reason to splurge—they last a long time, ultimately saving you money.

8. Don't just think green.

Make decisions with an eye on style, not just because it might be green. Ensuring that your stuff lasts, and buying things that can adapt over time, is actually very sustainable. I think of sustainable style as harkening back to how people used to live before mass production and our consumer economy changed it all. Being sustainable should make your life easier, not add a layer of complication. Although the current marketplace offers a limited selection of sustainable products, it is growing by the day. Unfortunately, until the supply of eco-products reaches the tipping point, many things like organic clothing and food may continue to be more expensive than the alternative. This book provides many ways to be eco-friendly without paying the high cost.

9. Step out of the box.

It's undeniable that the big-box stores make shopping easier and keep many people employed. And when they offer sustainable options, such as organic cotton clothing, they can move mountains. But what good is that when most of the stuff you buy falls apart, or doesn't fit well, or comes from a dubious manufacturing source? There will always be things that are easier to buy in a big-box retail store—underwear comes to mind. But sometimes we get lazy and buy at Target or Walmart simply because it's

easy and cheap: As you're walking around the store, you buy this and that because, oh, it's on sale, or it's really cute, or you just want it. Think of this book as a guide to help answer your shopping needs in a new way, outside of the box. I'll show you how to find or create quality items that are long-lasting, inexpensive, and sometimes just plain free.

10. Become a thrifter.

Thrift stores, flea markets, antique bazaars, and yard sales are the purview of people for whom "thrifting" is a verb. This person, the Thrifter, is inspired by what other people pass by: the little detail on the side of a teacup, the shine beneath the tarnish, the reflection dulled by the years. Thrifting is an opportunity to delve into someone else's life, to pass through the momentary interests or lifelong passions exhibited in the wares they offer. Thrifting is a very intimate experience—whether in a store or on a lawn, you are touching something that was used, and maybe loved, by someone else. The Thrifter loves the history, the experience, and the resilience of an old find newly acquired. There's another component for the Thrifter—the challenge of re-purposing something that somebody else has given up on. It's a creative im-pulse, the desire to recreate or repurpose something anew.

REPURPOSE

When resources such as tin, cork, wood, and glass were used to make our household items, repurposing was simply a fact of life. Using old milk jars on the table for fresh cut flowers made sense. Tearing up worn clothes to make braided rugs, or making baskets out of leftover wire from a chicken coop, was simply the smart thing to do. It wasn't unusual or exceptional. Nobody called you creative or crafty if you did any of these things. This also meant you probably had the necessary tools and materials to do these everyday projects, or else could borrow them from a neighbor. You might have a complete collection of Craftsman tools (lucky you), but just in case you don't, here's an overview of tools and materials to help with the projects in *Eco-Chic Home*— and maybe a few new projects I hope you'll dream up along the way.

TOOL BOX

Cutting Tools

> **Fabric Scissors** These are available with a plastic handle, which can be more comfortable when cutting fabric.

> **Paper Scissors** Paper dulls blades fairly quickly, which is why you want to keep two pairs on hand.

> **Paper Cutter** A tabletop paper cutter is very useful for craft projects; it will save your hands when you have a lot of cutting to do.

> **X-Acto Knife** Helpful when doing precise cutting projects. It's also good to have a straight edge (often a metal ruler with a rubber grip backing) to help guide your cutting.

> **Utility Knife** For cutting cardboard and other materials. It is best to get one with a retractable blade for safety. I also recommend wearing work gloves when using a utility knife.

> **Cutting Mat** Professional quality, self-healing cutting mats are indispensable for any crafter. They protect table surfaces and are designed for both rotary blades and straight utility blades.

> **Gardening Shears** Very helpful to trim things like twigs or even a small wooden dowel.

> **Wire Cutters** Helpful when you want to use wire in your projects, or when you need to take things such as picture frames apart.

- › **Metal Snips** Also called tin snips, these cut through aluminum or tin cans.
- › **Handheld Hole Punches** Get two sizes, one-quarter inch and one-eighth inch.
- › **Six-Inch Auto Center Punch (Awl)** Lets you punch holes in thin metal sheeting, leather, or stacks of paper. Get one with a guide. This is also a good tool to mark where you want to sink a nail or screw.
- › **Small Electric Saw** Should be used specifically for small projects, such as cutting through porcelain.
- › **Bone Folder** Not for cutting, but indispensible when working with paper and other materials.

Glue, Tape, and Staples
- › **Wood Glue** Super adhesive, good to help keep things in position before nailing or screwing together.
- › **Craft Glue** Works on fabric and paper.
- › **Mod Podge** The best product for decoupage projects. You can also make your own version by mixing together craft glue and water
- › **Gaffer's Tape** Available in craft stores, this is indispensable because it can be easily removed from any surface without leaving sticky residue. Also great for bookbinding projects.
- › **Glue Gun** Many crafters find this an indispensable tool. Get one that has multiple heat settings so you can use it on both delicate materials such as paper and fabric and more resilient items such as ceramic, plastic, and metal.
- › **Staple Gun** Very helpful for attaching fabric to wood. I love the Hitachi Narrow Crown Pneumatic Stapler. It's not too heavy and really packs a punch.
- › **Staple Remover**

Drills, Hammers, and Screwdrivers

›   **Electric Drill** Get a plug-in rather than a battery-operated drill, and
     make sure you have an assortment of different drill bit sizes. I find
     plug-in drills have more power; just keep an extension cord with the
     drill and you'll always be able to reach your project.
›   **Mallet** Useful when you want to sink a nail without denting the wood.
›   **Hammer**
›   **Screwdriver**

Sanding and Painting

› **Sandpaper** Use to smooth surface imperfections before painting.

› **Hand Sander** Makes sanding surfaces easier and faster.

› **Fine Steel Wool** Gets paint out of crevices.

› **Low-VOC Paint** VOCs are volatile organic compounds, and it's best to avoid them whenever possible.

› **Paint Sponge** Helps get paint into tricky angles and puts a lot of paint on a surface area really fast.

› **Paintbrushes**

› **Paint Roller**

› **Drop Cloth**

Sewing

› **Sewing Machine** You don't need to spend a lot to get a decent sewing machine, but if you do, it is well worth the investment. If you take good care of your machine, it really is something you could have for the rest of your life.

› **Sewing Needles** Look for an assorted pack it should have every size needle required.

› **Embroidery Needles** These have a blunt tip, so they're good for basic embroidery projects as well as for sewing through cardboard and stacks of paper.

› **Embroidery Thread** Just get the basic primary colors, along with white and black, and you should have everything you need for the most basic projects.

› **All-Purpose Thread** I prefer cotton; a medium weight will get you through practically any sewing task at hand.

› **Fabric Pencil** It's smart to mark your fabric before cutting. You can also use tailor's chalk. Either option will wash right off.

› **Straight Pins**

ENTRYWAY
Welcome Home

Organizing your entryway with the projects in this chapter will definitely help you with living greener. The entryway is sometimes a forgotten part of the house. Maybe you use the formal hall at the front, or maybe you always use the back door that opens into your kitchen. Wherever you enter and leave, chances are you keep some of the same things there, and tend to have the same pile-up of mail, keys, wallets, cell phones, etc. This chapter deals with keeping those important things better organized so that you don't have to search for your keys every day, or worse, lose items and have to replace them. There are also some easy ways to organize mail that I hope will encourage you to take action to reduce the amount of paper you receive in the mail in the form of magazines, catalogs, junk mail, and bills. Consider this your entryway to *Eco-Chic Home* and the many inventive ways you can repurpose everyday items into chic essentials you can't live without.

RECYCLED MAGAZINE BOWL

It can be a challenge to keep your entryway in order, but this recycled bowl project will help you organize and reduce that pile of magazines you may have stacked up. Strategically placed items like this bowl are a convenient way to keep track of the little things: your keys, loose change, subway or bus pass. Hopefully recycling magazines is already part of your daily living (luckily, most can be recycled). Even though the magazine industry is making strides toward greening their business and more publishers are using only Forestry Stewardship Council approved paper, finding a way to artfully reuse the magazines is the ideal solution. Now when you're done with your favorite magazine, recycling isn't your only option.

Tools and Materials

› 1 magazine
› 40 small butterfly clips
› Crafter's glue
› X-Acto knife
› Bone folder tool
› Paper cutter

How To

1. Use the X-Acto knife to cut out about 20 magazine pages. Keep steady pressure on the knife as you slice through the pages, and don't release pressure until you finish the cut. (X-Acto knife blades are pretty sharp, so you'll probably end up cutting out a few pages at a time.)
2. Next, cut each page in half lengthwise using your paper cutter.
3. Once you have a nice stack of paper (about 40 strips) to work with, take one piece and fold an edge over about 1 inch.

4. Use the bone folder to crease the fold, then continue folding over and over again until you reach the end, using the bone folder every few folds.
5. Put a butterfly clip at the ends of each piece to hold it together.
6. Make 40 folded pieces. You can make more later if needed.
7. To create a base for the bowl, take one folded magazine strip, with the open fold facing down, and roll it into a tight coil. Place dots of glue in between each part of the coil as you wind it together. You'll end up with a round disk.
8. Take a second folded piece (with the open fold facing down) and glue the end to the outside of the first disk. Roll this second piece around the disk, again placing dots of glue periodically in between each coil.
9. Continue adding pieces like this until you have an 8-inch-wide flat disk.
10. Place the next piece with the open fold facing up and away from the center disk.
11. Coil it around your 8-inch disk, using glue to keep it in place.
12. To create the sides of the bowl, take a piece with the open fold up and facing away from the center piece, but instead of gluing it to the outside as you have been doing, stick it inside of the last piece you attached. Use dots of glue to keep it in place, and be sure to leave about half of it sticking up and out of the piece it is going into.
13. Take the next piece and do the same thing, but this time place it into the piece that is sticking up. As you will see, this creates the gradual rise of the bowl.
14. Each new piece should fit nicely in the last piece. Remember to use the glue to hold each new piece in place.

ECO-BIT: WASTE OF TIME

The average American spends eight months of their life opening junk mail. The amount of junk mail received every day could produce enough energy to heat 250,000 homes (source: Oberlin College, 2008).

15. Continue to place each new piece so that you literally sculpt the bowl, piece by piece.
16. To make the final piece, which will be the rim of the bowl, place it in the last piece with the folded part down.

Note: You can use any type of paper for this project—newspaper, printer paper, notebook paper, and decorative paper will all work.

CLOTHESPIN FILING

Old-fashioned wooden clothespins have a definite charm, and they can be used around the house for many different projects. Use them in your entryway to keep mail sorted. I keep our mail in a basket and use clothespins to separate the bills, correspondence, and junk mail. I save all of our junk mail and when I have time, go online to request our names be removed from companies' mailing lists. As soon as you bring your mail inside, sort it with clothespins. Use a pen to write "bills," "personal," or "medical" on each clothespin. This way, you can keep your entryway uncluttered and organized until you have the time to tackle your to-do list.

BOOK KEEPER

Once you begin your mail-stopping campaign, you'll need to hang on to your junk mail and catalogs to enter the names and addresses of companies you wish to block. Until you have time to sit down with the junk mail at your computer to remove your name from mailing lists, this remade accordion file will keep them neatly tucked away. You might also store loose pieces of paper, shopping lists, or mail in this folder. The accordion stands up so you can find things fast and stash things easily. I like to use old book covers, because they typically fit a letter-size accordion file.

ECO-BIT: PAY ONLINE

If you still get bills in the mail, you can easily reduce your paper trail and make the switch to digital. Bank statements, credit card bills, even your utilities can all be paid easily and securely online.

Tools and Materials
› X-Acto knife
› 2 used hardback book covers, or pieces of medium-weight cardboard (cut to match the size of your accordion folder, usually 5 inches by 7 inches)
› Fabric remnants
› Fabric pen or chalk
› Pinking shears
› Spray adhesive
› Cutting mat
› Accordion file (letter size)
› 10 inches of 1-inch-wide grosgrain ribbon
› Straight edge
› Glue gun
› Sewing machine

How To

1. Lay the accordion file flat on top of a piece of cardboard. Make sure the source of cardboard is big enough for this project.
2. Using the straight edge, neatly trace an outline of the folder with a pen.
3. Remove the folder, and with the straight edge and X-Acto knife, cut out the cardboard pieces.
4. Put the cardboard to the side and lay the fabric remnant flat on the cutting surface.
5. Place one cardboard piece on top of the fabric and trace an outline with fabric pen or chalk.
6. Cut out two pieces of fabric, giving both a 3-inch seam allowance. Lay one piece of fabric flat.
7. Hold a piece of cardboard up with one hand and with the other hand apply spray adhesive to the one side.
8. Immediately place the cardboard firmly down on a fabric piece. Lay the fabric-covered cardboard fabric-side down.

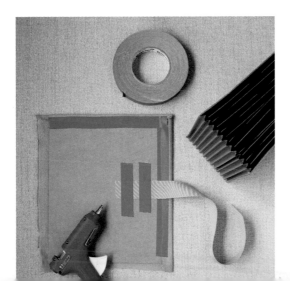

9. Put glue dots along one edge of the extra fabric, fold it over onto your cardboard and pull it tight, then smooth it out to remove gaps and bubbles.
10. Repeat steps 7 and 8 with the opposite side of fabric.
11. Glue down the top and bottom fabric edges until the cardboard is completely covered on one side.
12. Take 10 inches of ribbon and use the sewing machine to stitch one end so it does not unravel.
13. Glue the unsewn end to the cardboard, on the nonfabric side, so that 4 inches is adhered to the surface on one side exactly in the middle. You will be able to tie the folder shut with the ribbon.
14. Repeat steps 6 through 13 with the second side.
15. Place the folder on its side and tie the ribbons together, and you're done.

Note: You can just as easily use wallpaper remnants or newspaper for the wrapping. And this also works with larger accordion files.

ORDERLY DRAWERS

Get a drawer in order with this simple idea. Take an old muffin tin you no longer have use for, or pick one up at a flea market. Spray paint it, or leave it unpainted, it's entirely up to you. If you use paint, use enamel gloss paint. Add some fabric—velvet, satin, or felt—to the bottom of each compartment, and put it in a drawer. Instant organizer.

HANGING POCKET ORGANIZER

When a men's button-down shirt gets frayed at the collar and cuffs, it usually means it's no longer office-worthy. But you can repurpose the shirts to keep them working for you. This pocket organizer idea uses the breast pockets from well-worn shirts. If your entryway is on the small side, this is an ideal project because you can hang it on your wall or even the inside of a closet door. Not only does this give you another nice way to organize, you don't even need a table. It's a convenient place to put the little items that are so easily lost: For instance, if you have a dog, put the leash in one pocket and biodegradable poop bags in another—great for those times when your furry friend really has to go.

Note: You can use any shirt with a pocket, or even the back pockets from old blue jeans. Save the extra fabric from this project for the Fancy Hanger in the chapter titled "Bedroom."

Tools and Materials
›   Rotary cutter (or pinking shears)
›   Straight edge
›   Fabric pencil or chalk
›   6 men's dress shirts with breast pockets
›   Tape measure
›   Pins
›   Sewing machine
›   Iron and ironing board

How To

1. Draw a 5-inch-by-5-inch outline around each breast pocket with the straight edge and your fabric pencil.
2. Use the straight edge and the rotary cutter to cut along the outline you made around each breast pocket.
3. Fold a ½-inch hem all the way around each pocket square (hem should be on the nonpocket side). Press the hem flat with iron.
4. Sew a hem-stitch around each square on the sewing machine.
5. Lay one shirt flat with the button-hole side at the top of the cutting mat. You are going to leave the button holes on the fabric piece. Next cut a piece of fabric that is 15 inches by 15 inches for the backing, making sure that button holes are at the corner edges of the backing piece.
6. Fold a ½-inch hem around the sides and bottom of the backing piece, press, and sew a hem stitch.
7. Lay the squares side by side and top to bottom on the backing piece, button holes at the top. Pin the squares and backing together and sew together. Be sure to sew around each pocket to reinforce it.
8. Use the button holes to hang the organizer.

ECO-BIT: USED CLOTHING

When shopping in a thrift store, if you see an article of clothing made of good material such as cotton or wool, consider throwing it in your shopping bag. Even if you don't like the style or pattern, you can put it to good use with one of the projects in this book.

CLUTTER CONTAINED

A storage bin is a smart way to stash random items quickly and neatly. That way you can wait until you have time to put things in their proper home but don't have to look at a mess. In my home, we use these bins to store our shoes, which we remove when walking in the door. A storage bin is also a good place for you to keep recycling—mark one for glass, plastic, newspaper—for instant organization.

Tools and Materials
›   Cardboard box, about 16 inches wide, 15 inches high, and 13 inches deep
›   Flat cutting surface (big enough for your box)
›   Box cutter
›   Felt tip marker
›   Pinking shears
›   2 yards of fabric (42 inches wide)
›   2 yards of organic unbleached muslin
›   Straight pins

How To
1.   Lay the box on its side and cut off all four flaps using the box cutter. Move the box to the side. You can also just fold the flaps down.

2.   Lay the fabric flat on the cutting surface—if it's a print, that side should face down.

3.   Trace each side of the box onto the fabric with the marker. The outline should look like a flat box, with the bottom and four sides extending out from all four sides of the bottom piece.

4.   Cut the pattern out with pinking shears, leaving a ½-inch seam allowance all the way around.

5.   Lay the fabric pattern on top of the muslin and cut out a matching piece.

6.   Use your sewing machine to hem the outside edges of both the outside fabric and the muslin (just fold the edges once—you don't need finished edges).

7.   Pin together the sides of the fabric for the outside of your bin so it resembles a box. Stitch the sides together with your sewing machine.

8.   Put the box inside the fabric cover, then place the muslin lining inside. Lay the box on its side and stitch the two sides together on your sewing machine. When you finish one side, turn the box and sew that edge on the machine. Now your box is ready to help you contain your clutter.

MAGAZINE FILE BOX

Just because I don't subscribe to many magazines doesn't mean I don't have a pile waiting to read. I order used ones online—it saves a lot of money and is an excellent way to upcycle. I'm always happy to find a way to keep them around in an orderly fashion. This project makes good use of empty cereal boxes. To make this project, you'll need two empty cereal

HISTORY OF
MODERN
ART
PAINTING · SCULPTURE
ARCHITECTURE

H. H. ARNASON

あみぐるみの本 タカモリ・トモコ 日本ヴォーグ社

子どもだってきちんとした服 天然素材が気持ちいいね vol.2 3歳から8歳まで 小山千夏 文化出版局

ニューヨークの子ども服 ちいさな革・羊毛・毛糸で作ったひとつのもの作り 尾方裕司 文化出版局

GOURMET DECEMBER 2008

GOURMET MARCH 2009

GOURMET JUNE 2009

boxes of the same size, an X-Acto knife, a straight edge, a cutting mat, and some gaffer's tape.

First, open the top and bottom of one cereal box, then cut it open along one seam. Make sure you keep it in one piece so you can

ECO-BIT: TIME IS VALUABLE

Time may not be a natural resource, but it is a precious one. With more time, you can be more effective in your life, with more opportunities to adopt greener habits. More time also means you can take on the projects in this book. So treat your time like it is something to be respected rather than just frittered away.

reassemble it. Lay the box flat. Use a ruler to measure 6 inches down on both the left and right edges. On the left side of the box, place the ruler at a right angle, stopping at the first crease in the center. Cut the left corner with an X-Acto knife. Repeat on the right edge. Now reassemble the box with the printed part facing in. Use gaffer's tape to neatly tape the sides together. For the second box, just cut off the top flaps and put the box inside of the first box. Trim the front and sides of the box to match the outside one. Use gaffer's tape to tape the two boxes together and cover the trimmed edges. Your new magazine file is the perfect place to hold magazines until you have time to read them.

CLEVER CLOCK

Creating a schedule is one way to keep yourself better organized, and having a visual reminder of the time is a helpful way to stay on track. This project is an easy upgrade to your entryway and a clever way to repurpose a boring old wall clock. To paint this tongue-in-cheek homage to the classic grandfather clock, you will need an old wall clock—the kind you'd find in a classroom is ideal. You'll also need one pint of acrylic paint, one medium-

size and one small paintbrush, paint sealant, several pages of newspaper, hammer, and hanger for clock. Use a pencil to draw an outline of a grand-father clock (most grandfather clocks are at least six-feet tall and one-and-a-half-feet wide), making sure that your clock face fits into the outline. Use the small paintbrush to paint the outline and the medium paintbrush to fill in the body of the clock. Once the paint has dried, apply a coat of acrylic paint sealant. Hang your wall clock where the face of the grandfather clock should be. Just don't wait for it to chime!

BRAIDED RUG

Another aid against cold winter nights is this little rug project. I envision this next to a bed, a perfect spot for your slippers and maybe your dog, too. Wall-to-wall carpet was a true luxury in the 1950s when it first hit the market, before we realized the amount of pollutants absorbed by the fibers in the carpet. This braided rug project is a way to upcycle old clothes and it's easy to wash. Braided rugs have been around for ages, just one example of how people used to squeeze value out of every household item. If we still had to grow the cotton, spin the yarn, and make the clothing we wear, we'd probably be less likely to get rid of things, too. Don't have a stash of old T-shirts lying around the house? Hit your local thrift store. Use natural fabric dye if you want a specific color palette. Try to use the same type of fabric and the same thickness. You can easily use wool, just make sure all of it is the same thickness.

Tools and Materials
› Large, flat work area
› 20 cotton T-shirts
› Fabric scissors
› Sewing machine
› Cutting mat
› Painter's tape
› Embroidery needle
› Embroidery thread
› Straight pins

How To

1. Lay a T-shirt flat, cut the seams on each side all the way up to the arms. Trim off the arms and open the T-shirt flat on the cutting mat, with the neck opening in the middle. Cut the two pieces in half along the shoulder seams, and then cut the T-shirt lengthwise into 3-inch-wide strips. Repeat with the rest of the shirts.
2. Sew three strips of fabric together at one end.
3. Tape the sewn end to a flat surface with painter's tape and braid the three strips together.
4. When you complete the braid, finish the end by stitching it off with the sewing machine.
5. Repeat this process with all of the fabric pieces.
6. Begin coiling the rug at one end, keeping the coil flat on a table surface. If necessary, use straight pins to hold coil in place.
7. When you've coiled one entire braid, thread your embroidery needle and use it to lace over and under each braided piece, from right to left and top to bottom.
8. Repeat this process until all of the braids have been added, and you have a decent-size rug.
9. Stretch and flatten the rug, then place it on the floor.

LIVING ROOM
Think Small

We have become accustomed to larger homes—much larger. Did you know that the size of the average U.S. home has increased by 140 percent since the 1950s? All of that extra space saps energy and money. The result is a plague of high-energy-use homes across the country. In the United States, 40 percent of our energy use comes directly from petroleum. In this era of reducing, we need to rethink the size of our homes. If we use the space we have more efficiently, we won't feel like we don't have room for all of our stuff. One way to live more effectively with the space you have is to make such rooms as the living room more user-friendly and versatile. This chapter is about repurposing materials into things that will help you live more comfortably. All of the projects in this chapter are designed to help maximize space in a stylish and utilitarian way—the definition of eco-chic.

ECO-BIT: REMOVE YOUR SHOES

Shoes can track more than just dirt into your home. Pesticides, lead, and bleach are just a few of the pollutants you might bring inside with you. Removing your shoes at the door is a very easy way to keep your home cleaner and healthier.

EASY REUPHOLSTERED CHAIR

A traditional way to make furniture more user-friendly has always been the slipcover. In the past, people changed the slipcovers with the seasons. This project is somewhat similar to that idea, but instead it gives you a temporary solution to make over any chair. This is more like the cheater's version of upholstering, but is an easy way to convert an old chair into something you actually want to sit on. Upholstering is a craft that takes time to master; if you would like to learn, there may be a class offered at your local fabric store. As an alternative, this project offers a quick fix. Instructions are based on the chair pictured, but you can adjust them for basically any upholstered chair. If you're doing a total rehab like we did, you'll need sandpaper, paint, and a paintbrush. Unfortunately, our chair had some missing parts, so we opted to just remove all of the ornamental circles, fill in the nail holes with wood filler, and give it a fresh coat of paint.

ECO-BIT: SMALLER HOUSES
The motto of the Small House Movement is "to live simply so that others may simply live." This movement promotes smaller housing alternatives that are afforable and ecological. The Small House Society has ideas and resources at www.resourcesforlife.com.

Tools and Materials
› Upholstered chair
› 2 yards fabric (light canvas or textile-grade)
› Fabric pen or chalk
› Fabric scissors
› Measuring tape
› T-square (an interior designer/architect model is useful for measuring and outlining on fabric when making your own patterns)

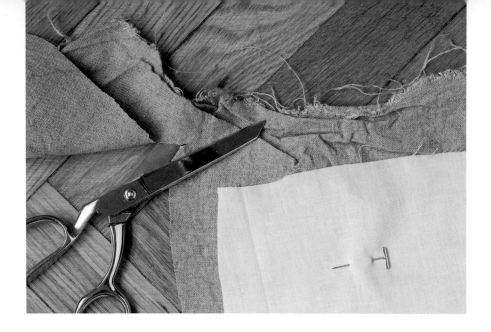

> › Iron and ironing board
> › Staple gun and staples
> › Safety glasses
> › Straight pins
> › Ornamental rounds trim (measure the edge and decide how much; it never hurts to have a little extra)
> › Sewing machine

How To

1. Measure the seatback cushion; be sure to include the curve in your width estimate, then measure the seat cushion.
2. Lay your fabric flat on the cutting surface; canvas or textile fabrics are the best choice for any upholstery project.
3. Using your T-square, draw the pattern for the seatback and the seat.
4. Cut out each piece, leaving a 2-inch seam allowance all the way around.
5. Line up the top fabric piece with your chair back. Pin the fabric piece to the chair; you should have 2 inches of extra fabric all the way around.

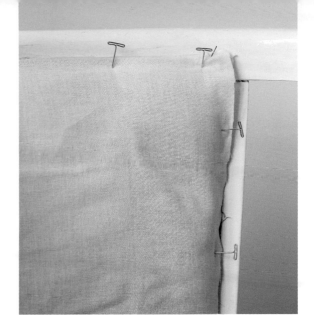

6. Repeat step 5 with the chair seat fabric. Remove both pieces of fabric.
7. Hem the top piece first. Fold about ½ inch on one side, iron it to make it crease, fold again, and press down with the iron. Repeat on all sides until entiro piece has a clean hem. Place the piece on the chair's back cushion one last time to be sure It is thc right size.
8. Stitch a hem all the way around on your sewing machine.
9. Repeat steps 7 and 8 with the seat fabric.

ECO-BIT: MDF

One of the best things about buying older, used furniture is that, unlike new furniture, it is not manufactured using medium density fiberboard (MDF). MDF results in poor quality pieces that will eventually disintegrate, so you won't be able to pass them down as family heirlooms. In addition to its poor quality, MDF is created using toxic compounds that are unhealthy for you and for the earth. When you do purchase something new, avoid MDF and opt for items made using real wood that has been forested sustainably.

ECO-BIT: PURCHASE TO REPURPOSE

When you decide to purchase a household item, ask yourself how can it be repurposed—is it a kitchen table that you can one day remake into a coffee table for your living room? Following this path, you might just find yourself purchasing less and saving more.

10. Use the staple gun to attach your new upholstery over the old chair. First, pin both pieces with straight pins. Place the pins so that you can staple right next to each one.
11. As you are pinning, gently pull the fabric taut so it is totally smooth. You want it to be as tight as possible once affixed permanently as it will stretch over time.
12. Put on your safety glasses and using the staple gun, staple the fabric directly to the old fabric underneath. Don't staple the wood in case you ever want to have the chair totally reupholstered at some point— you won't want a bunch of holes in the wood.
13. Use a hot glue gun to secure any ornamental rounds around the fabric edges. Cover all of the staples and the gap between the new fabric and the wood frame (if there is a gap).
14. Let the glue set overnight before you put the chair to work.

PILLOW BAND

This pillow band keeps your throw pillows clean and longer-lasting, as well as giving you the option to change things up once in a while. I like throw pillows, but they get dirty really fast in my house. Even if you can take the cover off and wash it, some stains just won't come off. The pillow band solves that problem and makes it easier to pile up the pillows. You will have a fabric sleeve that you can take off or put back on whenever you want. When you're at a thrift store, go ahead and buy those ugly throw pillows and turn them into something you adore.

To make this project, you will need a throw pillow, 1 yard of fabric (of course, this depends on the size of your pillow), scissors, a sewing machine, pins, iron and ironing board, a bone folder, and a yard of grosgrain

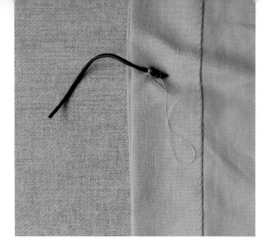

ribbon or rawhide to tie the open ends together. This is also a great project for using up fabric remnants.

Take a piece of fabric and lay it flat, then place the pillow you want to cover on top of the fabric. Trace an outline of the pillow at the top and bottom on the fabric piece. Fold the piece of fabric in half and cut enough to cover the pillow one time. Leave a 2-inch seam allowance. You are making a band of fabric that slips over the pillow, so you will sew only one seam. Two sides will be left open. Fold one edge over a ½-inch; crease it with the bone folder, then iron the crease in place. Sew the hem closed. Do this all the way around all four sides of your fabric. Bring the two ends of fabric together, turn the fabric inside out, and sew the ends together. Turn the fabric right-side out. Slip it on to your pillow. Now, instead of getting rid of pillows that don't jibe with your new design direction, just sew a few bands of fabric and slip them over the pillows for an instant change.

FILE DRAWER SIDE TABLE

This project takes the idea of repurposing to the next level by transforming something you may never have liked into something useful and attractive enough to put in your living room. Whenever possible, see if you can use things for more than one purpose. Purchasing used office furniture is a great way to save money and resources, but you must be willing to look beyond the bland appearance. An unbelievable amount of used office furniture is available for very little money, including the classic but ugly metal filing cabinet. Chances are good that a filing cabinet like this one has been a part of your life at some point. I doubt anyone actually likes the way they look, but they're very useful. Not to worry, this quick conversion can remake the good old filing cabinet in a chic way so it won't be something you merely tolerate.

Tools and Materials

› 1 used two-drawer file cabinet
› Measuring tape
› 1 piece of ¼-inch thick plywood, cut to the same size as the top of the file cabinet (this will give you a strong tabletop)
› Fabric scissors
› 2 yards of fabric (use repurposed sheets or drapes if you can)
› Iron and ironing board
› Sewing machine

Note. You'll make two separate finished fabric pieces, one to drape over the front of the cabinet, the second to drape over the side of the cabinet. This will give you two openings in the front on either side of the cabinet for easier access to the drawers. Otherwise you would need to lift the entire skirt up if you ever wanted to open one of the drawers.

How To

1. Measure the filing cabinet: Begin with the front and measure from the floor to the top, continue measuring across the top toward the back of the cabinet, and finally down the back to the floor. This will be for your first piece. Repeat this step with the side of the cabinet.

2. Cut out two separate fabric pieces using the measurements you took, adding a 2-inch seam allowance on all sides.
3. Sew a hem on the ends of the first piece. Fold the side edges, and iron a crease, then fold again and make another crease.
4. Repeat step 3 with the second piece.
5. Take your precut piece of plywood and place it on top of the bare file cabinet.
6. Lay each piece of fabric, overlapping, to cover the wood top and the file cabinet.

Note: If you want the option of moving the table (or to make it a little higher), add a set of casters to the four bottom corners using an electric drill, nuts, and bolts.

ECO-BIT: NATURAL FURNITURE CLEANER

The best way to keep furnishings looking nice is to regularly clean them. Frequent little spurts of cleaning are much more effective than the occasional blitz. This natural solution makes that even easier because you can make it yourself. The solution works for upholstered furniture, rugs, drapes, wood, tile, stone, or cork flooring. You will need a clean rag (an old cloth diaper is also good), a vacuum cleaner, a stiff-bristled broom, a large rubber band, and a 1-pint spray bottle. First, vacuum loose dirt and debris from upholstered furniture or rugs. Wrap the clean rag over the end of a stiff-bristled broom and hold In place with a rubber band. Fill the spray bottle with one part white vinegar and four parts water. Spray the area you're cleaning and then lightly run the rag-covered broom over the area. Don't scrub; just wipe the broom a couple of times over the area. Make sure the surface dries in just a few minutes (if it doesn't, wipe with the broom again). Keep your furniture, rugs, and pillows clean and toxin-free with this natural, homemade cleaning solution—it's less harsh on fabric and wood, and healthier for you.

FELT COASTERS

The coaster is one of those simple things you need to take care of your furniture. They may be utilitarian, but that doesn't mean they can't add some style to your space, too. Skip the disposable coaster next time you have a party; this simple felt project can provide you with as many coasters as you have friends. A wool sweater thrown into a superhot washing machine becomes felt fabric that you can turn into many different

ECO-BIT: WATER-STAINED TABLE

Oops, someone didn't use a coaster. Don't get rid of a coffee table, or pass up a used one, just because of a few water marks. To remove a water stain from a wood surface, run a hot iron on a smooth-textured, lint-free cloth placed on top of the stain. Iron very briefly (only a few seconds), lift the cloth, and repeat until the stain is gone. Making repairs like this to furniture is a great way to keep items out of the waste stream, and save a little money, too.

things. (See the Natural Centerpiece in the chapter titled "Dining Room" for another felt project.) To make coasters, just take a wool sweater (it must be wool, not acrylic or cotton) and throw it in the washing machine on the hottest setting. Wash the sweater three times this way, then let it dry overnight. The next day, lay the sweater flat and simply trace around a large mug, and then cut the circles out. That's it—instant coaster. Cheers!

Note: Different types of felt can be created by using a different number of washings: The more you wash the sweater, the tighter the weave becomes. We found that three times is the right number for this coaster project, because the coaster should be thick enough to protect the table's surface.

MILK PAINT TABLE

Maybe you have a piece of furniture with bigger problems than just a water stain—before you toss it or hide it away, make some milk paint and bring it back to life. Milk paint is one of the oldest kinds of paint, it's totally natural, and it can be used to paint almost anything. Since you don't have to buy paint at the store, it's extra easy to upgrade anything fast—I dragged this table in off the street. Dumpster-diving may not be for everyone. But just like the rag-and-bone men who created the original Paris Flea Market, dumpster-divers don't look at what an item is—they see what it might be. Dumpster-diving is an adventure you can take every time you leave the house. The rules are simple: If you see something on the curb, it's fair game. Then when you bring something home, make some milk paint and turn that trash into treasure.

Tools and Materials

To make milk paint:
› Gallon skim milk
› 2 cups white vinegar
› ¼ cup hydrated lime powder (type S, available in craft stores)
› ½ cup pigment powder (if you want a color other than white, find this at craft stores; the powder must be lime-proof)

To paint the furniture:
› Sandpaper
› Painter's cloth
› Old piece of furniture, such as a table
› Paint pan
› Paint roller
› Rag

> › Paintbrushes in varying sizes
> › Damp rag

Making the Paint
1. Mix the milk and the lime together, stirring until there are no lumps.
2. Add the vinegar and the powdered pigment to create desired color. The vinegar will keep the milk from causing mold, which is a good thing.

Keep paint in the refrigerator; milk paint will keep for two to three days this way.

Painting the Furniture
1. Put furniture over a painter's cloth. Lightly sand the entire surface area to remove dirt and debris and give you a smooth surface. If your piece is laminated wood, sanding will help the paint stick to the surface.
2. Wipe the surface down with a damp rag. Allow for drying time; a few hours should be fine.
3. Use a medium-size paintbrush to apply milk paint, or a roller if the item has a bigger surface area (the side of a dresser, for example).
4. Let the paint dry overnight before you use the furniture. Depending on the piece, you may also need to apply a second coat of paint.

FLOOR CUSHION

Floor cushions are an underappreciated item; you can sit on them, lie on them, or put a tray on top for an instant table. This project's genius is that you can arrange old sleeping pillows any way you want: Tie them all together and lay them flat (sleeping), stack them and put a tray on top (table), or make two separate floor cushions (sitting). You might also decide to use them as throw pillows on your couch. Almost any fabric will do; I used fabric from a vintage skirt belonging to my mom. I loved the fabric but I didn't want to wear it—now I can enjoy the fabric, and my floor cushion, at the same time.

Tools and Materials

› 5 yards fabric (find remnants in your fabric store, or repurpose something like my skirt)
› 2 standard, firm bed pillows
› Fabric pencil or chalk
› Fabric scissors
› Iron and ironing board
› Pins
› Sewing machine
› Tape measure

ECO-BIT: REDUCE, REUSE, REARRANGE

Instead of buying new things when you want a change, give your home an instant style makeover by rearranging what you have. Move rugs, chairs, and lamps around a room, or even trade things from one room to another. Repurpose items in a creative way. I like to use some of my nicer things in unusual ways, like a crystal bowl that holds napkins on my table, or the vintage chicken egg cups that sit on my desk to hold paperclips, tacks, and whatever is small enough to fit in them. Pull things out of hiding in your closets and put them to work—you'll see that you can use practically everything in multiple ways, and give your home a fresh look without spending any money at all.

Note: This project is similar to the Pillow Band project. You will sew only two sides of the pillow covers; the two open sides of each covered pillow will have ties to close them and to connect them to another pillow.

How To

1. Place ½ yard of fabric flat on the floor.
2. Place two pillows side by side, and then draw an outline with your fabric pencil or chalk around both.
3. Fold the fabric piece in half, cut out four pieces of the pillow covers (you can cut two at once with the fabric folded). You will now have four pieces of fabric.
4. Repeat Steps 1 through 3 with your second ½ yard of fabric, but make the pieces 6 inches wider on the longest edge of the case. These will be longer than the first set of cases because you will use the extra fabric to cover the exposed pillow on either side. You should have eight pieces of fabric, which will become four pillow covers.
5. To make two fabric ties for each side (the long sides will be left open) of your pillow covers, cut out two 6-inch long, 3-inch wide strips of fabric. Sew a hem around each piece (you can just fold the edges once, iron them down, and then stitch), then sew each piece together so the hemmed part is in and you end up with a finished piece that will be a pillow tie. For each pillow you make, you'll need a total of eight ties. If you have four pillows, that's thirty-two ties. Sounds like a lot, but these are very easy to make.
6. Now sew finished hems all the way around each side of the pillow cover.

7. Line up two pieces of fabric on your cutting surface; place the wider piece down and the narrower piece on top. Pin the pieces together and sew the top and the bottom, but leave the sides open.

8. Attach four ties on each side (the longer side). Do this by folding the long piece of fabric in, making it even with the top, attach one tie 2 inches from the top and 2 inches from the bottom. Attach the corresponding ties to the top piece of fabric. Repeat on the other opening, and for all other pillows.

9. Now you can place your pillows inside their new covers, cover the pillow sides with the long piece of fabric on each side, and tie together. All of the pillows can be tied together and stacked, or you can used two tied together flat on the floor. You can even use these by themselves as throw pillows.

ECO-BIT: BUYING HANDMADE

I learned a lot about quality craftsmanship from working with incredibly talented designers in the fashion industry. Checking the seams is easy, but with mass production, it is difficult to know under what conditions an item was made, and such information is very complicated to trace. You don't have to worry about this with handmade goods, because more than likely, you are buying items directly from the producer. This is an easy way to be green, because handmade quite often means well-made.

KITCHEN
Think Fresh

Your kitchen is more than just a place to store and prepare food. Today's home basically revolves around the kitchen, with kitchen upgrades being the number one home remodeling project. Remodeling a kitchen can cost fifty thousand dollars (and that's at the low end) to one hundred thousand dollars. Real estate agents will tell you that remodeling a kitchen will bring the most value to the resale price of your home. This may be true, but only if the people buying your house like the choices you made. When it comes to design choices for the kitchen, people often do things that are trendy and of the moment, which makes a kitchen's design relevant for a finite period of time. The next family will most likely update it again. You can save a lot of money and waste if you stick to classic choices for things like countertops. They will stand the test—and changing tastes—of time.

CABINET DO-OVER

Ripping out kitchen cabinets is a big task, and unfortunately, if you want the cabinets to be reused (by someone else), it can be very expensive to keep them intact. Maybe you don't need to remove your cabinets at all.

ECO-BIT: THE BUSINESS OF RECYCLING

You might think that everything you send to recycling, including old kitchen cabinets, will be recycled into something else. Actually, this is not always the case. While items you send to the recycling plant are often turned into new materials that are then sold, for the recycling system to work, the monetary value of the materials must be high enough to give businesses an incentive to go to the expense of recycling. In economically difficult times, the value of recycled material can drop so much that businesses curtail their recycling programs. The reality is that cost, not environmental common sense, plays the biggest role in how and what communities choose to recycle, and sometimes it makes better fiscal sense for them to dump material than to recycle it.

I am of the opinion that people are much too quick to rip out old cabinets when a makeover will do fine. Simple door finishes are a subtle way to add polish. You can purchase moldings that can be easily adhered to any door for instant charm. This project is a lot cheaper—and greener—than replacing those kitchen cabinets.

Tools and Materials
› Screwdriver
› Pencil
› Decorative molding and appliqué pieces
› Plain cabinet doors
› Saw and miter box
› Paintbrush
› Primer
› Paint
› Wood glue
› Hammer

> Finish nails with small head
> Nail setter
> Wood filler

How To
1. Remove cabinet doors with a screwdriver. With a pencil, mark the placement of the moldings on the door.
2. Mark the molding with a pencil where cuts should be made.
3. Cut the pieces with a saw and miter box. (Or take the molding to a hardware store to have it cut.)
4. Prime and paint both the door and the molding; let dry.
5. Arrange the molding on the door, making sure to get a tight fit where the pieces meet at the corners.
6. Adhere the pieces to the door with wood glue and let sit for a half-hour or so.
7. Use a hammer and finish nails to attach each piece of the molding. Finish the nails with a nail setter.
8. Use wood filler to fill the nail holes and any gaps at the corners.
9. Apply another coat of paint to the door and the molding.
10. Replace the doors and admire.

INDUSTRIAL INSPIRATION

When looking for things that won't give your kitchen a dated look, think about adding some pieces from the industrial design era. The simple lines and utilitarian function of vintage factory accessories are timeless and easy to repurpose in your home. While there are certainly pricey options out there, you can find a wide variety of industrial items at affordable prices.

ECO-BIT: ENERGY STAR APPLIANCES

One thing I don't recommend holding on to are old appliances. If you
haven't switched your old kitchen appliances to energy-efficient models,
then you are literally throwing money out the window. Old appliances
probably cost more in energy than it would take to buy new appliances.
Today's dishwashers are about 95 percent more energy-efficient than those
bought in 1972, and a refrigerator built twenty years ago uses 70 percent
more energy than today's models (source: Environment Canada, 2007).

Flea markets and specialty hardware stores often have a good selection,
selling reclaimed items once used in offices, factories, even hospitals. The
simple design makes them easy to use. If you get your hands on a vintage
bathroom towel bar, attach it to the inside of a cabinet for a great place
to stash cookware. You might also be able to repurpose industrial lighting
fixtures in the kitchen, especially because they will provide excellent direct
light for cooking.

CREAMER AND SUGAR JAR

Even when kitchen appliances, dishes, or other things break or you lose a part, that doesn't mean you have to send them packing. I had a coffee maker for many years that always worked just fine. Then one day, the most important part—the coffee filter—went missing. I realized that when tak en apart, the two pieces make pretty great milk and sugar containers. I'm sure you have things in your kitchen just like this, and if you look at them a little differently, you can find a way to repurpose them like I did.

For this project, I simply cleaned the metal surface, then used painter's tape to cover the handle and knob up to the lid. Then I sprayed the entire surface area of both pieces with protective enamel. I found a spare lid from a glass jar that fit on the sugar container. Now I have a set that I couldn't have purchased anywhere in the world.

DIY DISH CLOTHS

Believe it or not, it wasn't long ago when people wouldn't have dreamed of using paper to clean up a mess. This project is a nice way to repurpose another household item—your old bath towels.

To make, find a clean surface to put a cutting mat. Lay the towel you're going to remake flat on the mat. Fold it over and cut the towel in half. You can use a dish cloth you already have as your pattern. Place your old cloth on top of the towel, matching up the left edge and upper left corner with the old towel. Use a ruler and fabric pencil to make your outline. Cut out the new dish cloths with pinking shears. Sew a finishing stitch all the way around each new dish cloth, skipping the edges that are already finished. For each dish cloth, you will need 8 inches of grosgrain ribbon for

ECO-BIT: STOP SPONGING

Sponges are made from cellulose sheets, which are made from tree
fiber. This material is mixed with cotton, molded, rinsed with an
antibacterial wash, then packaged (usually in plastic). There are
eco-friendly, biodegradable alternatives, such as the Twist Loofah
Sponge (greenhome.com).

a hanging loop. The ribbon should be no more than 2 inches wide. Wash the ribbon before using it for this project, but don't cut the individual loops until after you've washed it—you don't want it to unravel. Cut multiple 8-inch pieces with the pinking shears until you have enough for each new dish cloth. Fold one piece of ribbon in half, then match the ends of the ribbon to the right-hand corner of a dish cloth. The ribbon ends should be about 2 inches below the corner edge of the dish cloth. Attach the loop with a finishing stitch. Now that you have these adorable dish cloths, breaking that paper towel habit should be easy.

ECO-BIT: BEYOND PAPER TOWELS

Worldwide, the equivalent of about 270,000 trees are used and discarded each day. The biggest culprits are paper towels, napkins, facial tissues, and toilet paper. If every household in the United States reduced their consumption by just one roll of paper towels a year, we could save 1.4 million trees.

HANDMADE SPICE RACK

Talented cooks understand the importance of using spices to creating flavorful meals. Experimenting with spices can add another layer of interest to the cooking process. Give yourself another incentive to cook meals at home with this spice rack project. Any small drawer or wooden box can be remade as a perfect spice rack with the addition of a wooden shelf.

Get a piece of wood from the hardware store and have it cut to fit the width and depth of the drawer or box you want to use. If you are using a drawer, remove the handles or knobs and fill the holes with wood filler. After the filler dries, sand the newly filled surface smooth. Turn the drawer with the front panel facing down. Affix two small wooden or metal shelf brackets to the insides of the drawer. Paint the drawer, the brackets, and the shelf all one color. Place your shelf on the brackets. Attach two hanging hooks to the back of the new spice rack and hang it up in your kitchen. Fill with spice jars and start cooking.

JAR GLASSES

Glass may be one of the most recyclable materials, but you can do one better and save energy by repurposing those glass jars you use every day. Turn a random assortment of jars into quirky drinking glasses by removing the labels. Simply place the jars in boiling water for a few minutes. Then remove labels and most of the glue with soapy water. Use a little vegetable oil to remove the last little bit of glue. You can also paint your jar glasses using food-safe paint, such as Pebeo Porcelaine 150 paint. This paint dries after just ten minutes in a 300-degree F oven. After the pieces are completely cool, apply a gloss glaze to the dry jars. Allow to dry again before putting them to use.

CHIC PLASTIC SHOPPER

Although people may not cook from scratch anymore, that doesn't mean they aren't buying food. The truth is, much of what Americans eat comes in a box and goes in the microwave. To make matters worse, often what they buy comes home in the ubiquitous plastic bag. The plastic bag has become a part of our landscape, clogging waterways, choking wildlife, and littering practically every inhabited corner of our planet. But no matter how diligent we may be, somehow, some way, we all seem to accumulate our own fair

ECO-BIT: RECYCLING GLASS

Glass is extremely durable—it can be recycled forever. Recycling glass has enormous benefits: For every ton of glass recycled, we save an equivalent ton of resources. Glass recycling programs are also extremely successful. States with bottle deposit laws have 35 percent less litter than states without bottle redemption (source: EPA, 2008).

share of the omnipresent plastic bag. Maybe someday we will tell our children's children about the bags that once littered our landscape (let's hope). In the meantime, this project is a clever way to make use of these bags, since it takes about a billion years for one to decompose.

Tools and Materials

› Scissors
› 20 plastic shopping bags
› Thin piece of cardboard (12 inches by 6 inches)
› Craft scissors
› Fabric scissors
› 4 yards unbleached muslin
› Tote bag to use as a pattern (mine was a leather bag my grandmother brought back from Brazil thirty years ago)
› 1 roll parchment paper
› Iron and ironing board
› Embroidery needle
› Embroidery thread
› Glue
› Sewing machine

ECO-BIT: URBAN TUMBLEWEED

As of 2007, only 1 percent of plastic bags are recycled worldwide, and only 2 percent are recycled in the United States (source: www.salon.com).

How To

1. Choose your shopping bags. Cut the handles and the bottom off of each bag. To make this easy, roll the bag up so you have one long piece, then snip off the bottom and the top. Turn each bag inside out.

2. Place a piece of parchment that is slightly larger than your bags flat on the ironing board.

3. Lay five bags in a stack on top of the parchment. If you want to have any printing on your bag show up, take the second bag from the top and turn it right-side out. Lay an inside-out bag on top of that bag. You don't want to iron directly on the printing or you'll end up with a giant mess.

4. Put another piece of parchment paper on top of your stack of bags. It should be 2 inches larger on all sides so you won't iron directly on the plastic.

5. Turn your iron on the highest setting (mine is Acrylic but yours might be different) and open a window. Use a fan to draw air outside (there

may be fumes from the bags; while they're not too intense, you might want to keep this in mind—not very eco-friendly, I know).

6. Run the iron over the stack for about 30 seconds. Check to see if your bags have fused; if not, you can iron for a little while longer. Do not allow the bags to get too hot; you should periodically stop ironing and let them cool. Repeat steps 2–6 until you have the equivalent of about 3 yards of plastic material.

7. Lay muslin fabric flat. Take your "inspiration" bag and lay it flat on the muslin. Trace an outline of all sides of the bag, including the bottom, on the muslin, plus 2 inches for seam allowance.

8. Cut out all of the pieces—these will be your pattern. Lay each muslin piece on the plastic material, cutting out matching pieces of the plastic fabric.

9. Sew all four plastic pieces (but not the bottom) of your bag together with your sewing machine.

10. Turn the sewn piece inside out and sew the bottom of the bag with all seams facing in.

11. Cut out eight muslin pieces, approximately 8 to 10 inches wide, with a length that matches the width of your planned bag. These will create a "pocket" through which the bag's handles will run.

12. Lay the muslin pieces in a stack on a flat surface. Find the top-center, measure 2 to 4 inches out to each side, and draw a line to the bottom-center; then measure 4 inches up from that bottom-center point. Draw a U-shape, using the marks you just made as a rough guide. Keeping the pieces in a stack, cut this shape out of all muslin pieces.

ECO-BIT: CANNED FOOD

Almost all aluminum cans are lined with a thin layer of epoxy resin to keep the can from rusting. This resin is made from bisphenol A (BPA), which may be harmful when ingested, but there are no research studies completed as of yet. As a precaution, the U.S. government has begun to mandate that BPA not be used in any products intended for children (bottles, toys, pacifiers, etc.). If you need one more reason to eat fresh, locally produced food, then this is a pretty good one—so can the cans and eat fresh.

13. Hem all pieces on all sides, then sew two pieces together, matching up sides with hems facing in. Repeat. You should now have four sewn pieces.
14. Sew two pieces together, leaving a 2-inch opening near the top of each side of the U to feed the handles through.
15. For the bag handles, braid a few plastic bags together; the finished braids should be about 6 inches wider than your bag.
16. Sew the final two muslin pieces to top of the plastic bag on both sides. Feed both handles through the sleeves in the muslin and tie a knot at each end to keep the handles in place.

HANGING FRUIT AND VEGETABLES

Not only is it healthier and better for the environment to use farm-fresh ingredients, but it also adds flavor to your kitchen, especially if you have a nice way to display your fruits and vegetables. This hanging storage solution makes more room in your kitchen and gives you a visual reminder of the yummy (fresh) food waiting for you to eat. All you need are some cake tins or colanders and some thin chain or other material from which to hang your new storage.

Tools and Materials

› Electric drill
› 3 round cake tins, colanders, or similar
› Metal primer and paintbrush
› Gloss enamel spray paint
› Wire cutters
› 3 yards of small metal chain (or heavy twine or wire)
› 9 medium S-hooks
› 1 large S-hook
› Pliers
› Reinforced hook (for ceiling)

How To

1. Drill three holes, evenly spaced around the edges of each of three cake tins.
2. Paint the tins with a layer of metal primer. Let dry.
3. Apply a coat of spray paint over the entire surface of each tin. Let dry.
4. Use wire cutters to cut the chain into three equal pieces.
5. Attach an end of chain to each hole in the bottom tin using the medium S-hooks.
6. About one-third of the way between the bottom pan and the top of the chains, use three more S-hooks to connect the middle tin to the chains.
7. Halfway between the middle chain and the top of the chains, connect the top tin to the chains.
8. Squeeze the S-hooks shut with pliers.
9. Connect the top ends of the three chains with the large S-hook.
10. Hang the basket from a reinforced hook in the ceiling.

Note: You can also use graduated sizes of cake tins, with the largest on the bottom and the smallest on the top, or feature just one lovely piece.

REUSABLE SNACK CARRIER

It's true that plastic has its purposes, and one of them is taking food to go. Rather than throwing away last night's leftovers, pack yourself a lunch instead. This project lets you be green and practical at the same time. Just like you did with the Chic Plastic Shopper project, turn those plastic bags into something you can use again and again.

Use the same technique as in the Chic Shopper project. First make the plastic fabric using the fusing steps, then use your straight edge and a marker to draw a 12-inch-by-24-inch rectangle. Next, make a flap: Find the center of the rectangle and draw a 24-inch line. Make a 90-degree angle with your ruler at the top of the line, then do the same thing on the opposite side. The finished piece will resemble an envelope. Cut the pattern out with scissors. Fold the bottom up 12 inches; create a crease with a bone folder. With the iron and two pieces of parchment paper, fuse the two side edges of your envelope together. Fold down the flap, using the bone folder to make the crease. Use your glue gun to attach Velcro so the flap stays shut.

UTENSIL HOLDER

Use those old cans for adorable utensil holders. These containers can be used to set the table every day, and are also a nice way to display cutlery for an indoor or outdoor event. Making this tole-inspired utensil holder turns your aluminum can cast-offs into nice accessories for your kitchen. The word "tole" comes from the French, meaning lacquered or enameled metalware. It also means "table" or "board." Tole was a popular material for household wares in France during the sixteenth century. Today, antique tole items are quite expensive, but it's easy enough to create your own version of the classic French designs.

Save metal food containers—anything from coffee cans to soup cans will work for this project. Soak the container in hot water to help remove labels and any adhesive from the outside of the can. Spray the can with a layer of enamel paint. Let dry. Use a hammer and an awl to poke small holes in the sides if you'd like to make the can into a bucket. Fashion a handle from ribbon or a piece of wire. Place your utensils in the can, et voilà!

TRAY CHIC

Make setting the table easier and have a tray preset with all of your essentials. This project is another ingenious way to reuse smaller drawers by turning them into handled trays. The beauty of this project is that trays can be stacked if you want to put your table-setting essentials—napkins, utensils, salt and pepper—on different trays. You can never have too many trays—I have about a dozen in my house and find them indispensable. Various other cast-off items, once repurposed, make great trays: Old baking sheets, box lids, or old mirrors are just a few things looking for a second chance.

Tools and Materials
› 1 old shallow drawer that's on the smaller side (you don't want the tray to be too heavy to carry)
› Screwdriver (to remove old handles)
› 2 feet of ½-inch rope (for handles)
› Sandpaper
› Damp rag
› Primer
› Paint
› Medium-size paintbrush

- › No-VOC water sealant
- › 2 or 4 round metal ball feet
- › Wood glue
- › Electric drill
- › Ruler
- › Black felt tip marker

How To

1. Remove any handles from the drawer.
2. Turn the drawer over, and attach two metal ball feet to the back corners of the drawer (opposite from the side that had the handle). If your drawer is already level, with no leading front edge, then use 4 metal feet in all corners.
3. Mark the handle placement on both ends using the ruler and felt pen; this is where your new rope handles will go. Your rope handles will be placed about midway along the ends of the drawer, at least 1 inch from the top. Each handle should be about 4 inches wide. Drill four half-inch sized holes.
4. Smooth the surface of the drawer with sandpaper. Wipe the drawer clean with the rag.
5. When the wood is dry, paint a coat of primer on the drawer, inside and out, and on the bottom. Allow to dry.
6. Apply a coat of paint. You can apply a second coat to get the desired color if necessary. Allow to dry.
7. Reattach any original door handles (this really doesn't serve a purpose, but it's a nice touch).
8. Cut the rope in half. Feed both ends of one piece through the two holes on one side. Tie a knot in each end so you create a handle on the outside of the tray. Be sure you leave enough rope to fit your hand. Repeat this step on the opposite side, and you're ready to serve.

DINING ROOM
Set the Table

The dining room is a part of the home we should all become reacquainted with, so slow down and have a seat. We can all do a little better when it comes to making mealtime a priority. Taking the time to sit down to a meal with family or friends is an essential part of being healthy. Focusing on the importance of mealtime is also good for the environment—it is the core tenet of the local food movement, which started thirty years ago when Alice Waters opened Chez Panisse and simultaneously began her quiet crusade to keep farm-fresh ingredients available and in demand. Waters has since inspired community gardens, healthy school-meal plans, and dozens of other garden-focused initiatives. One of the first things Michelle Obama did when she moved into the White House was to plant a kitchen garden right on the South Lawn to showcase her support of healthy, locally grown food. With that spirit in mind, the projects in this chapter are meant to inspire you to embrace the art of entertaining and to rediscover the joy of cooking.

REMADE DISHWARE

Setting a nice table goes hand in hand with serving a delicious meal. Finding special things to set your table with might be as easy as opening the cabinet doors. You may have a complete set of fine china to work with—if so, use it! Fine china is one of my favorite things, and I don't think people use it enough. Personally, I have much more dishware than I can really use. My collection is made up almost entirely of secondhand pieces from both of my grandmothers. I also have many lonely teacups and saucers I rescued from thrift stores. As a result, there is a lot of mismatching going on. This project is a great way to turn any collection of random pieces into a matching set. You can create cohesion with one simple design. Make your design out of construction paper, or use a stencil to transpose the design onto the plates. Letters, numbers, animals, flowers, circles, fleur de lis, stars, and other designs are options. For this project, I used letter stencils.

ECO-BIT: SLOW FOOD

The Slow Food movement began in 1989 as a way to champion the notion of home-cooked meals, fresh ingredients, and gathering around the dinner table with regularity.

Tools and Materials

› Stencils
› Scissors (if you need to cut out your stencil)
› Assorted porcelain plates (can be totally mismatched)
› Felt tip marker, approximately the same color as your paint
› Small paintbrush
› Pebeo Porcelaine 150 (food-safe ceramic paint)
› Refillable butane torch
› Safety glasses
› Gloves

How To

1. Place the stencil on the plate surface and draw an outline on the plate with the pen.

2. Apply paint by tracing the outline of the design, then fill in the design using short, steady strokes over the surface of the plate and the design. You can either paint the inside of the design, or you can paint the outside and leave the design unpainted. Allow the paint to dry for about three hours.

3. Carefully use a butane torch to fire the plate (which will seal the design on the plate's surface). *You must be outside to use the torch.* Place the plate on a flat, outdoor surface such as cement, flat stone,

or bare ground (but do not place on grass). Wear protective eyeglasses, gloves, and keep hair tied back securely.

4. Set the torch on low and hold it so the flame is about 6 inches from the plate's surface. Slowly move the flame over the plate's surface just once. Don't let it get so hot that the paint gets bubbly.

5. Repeat this process a few more times, then leave plates to dry overnight. You may need to use the torch more than once to completely fire each plate.

Note: If you use a torch to fire the plates, they will be food and dishwasher safe, but don't use them in the microwave.

MISMATCHED TABLE

If painting plates isn't on your to-do list, you can create harmony with a collection of mismatched china in other simple ways. It takes very little to create a beautiful table setting; even with random pieces, one or two common elements can make it all come together. Choose one unifying detail—such as white teacups or plates. You might tie a sweet bow around

ECO-BIT: THE 100-MILE DIET

In 2007, Alisa Smith and J.B. McKinnon spent an entire year eating only food that was grown and produced within 100 miles of where they lived. The result was their groundbreaking book *Plenty*, chronicling their journey and providing a very real antidote to the megamart food-shopping experience dominating our culture.

each teacup handle using the same ribbon. Adding fresh fruit like oranges or lemons, coupled with bright flowers, will create an exciting synergy. I use random ephemera such as ribbon, gift tags, rocks, glass jars, buttons, and beads to put together a whimsical tablescape. It doesn't take much to add a little magic, just some pretty things and your imagination.

CREATIVE COMPOTES

Since you will be serving more fruits and vegetables, you'll need more ways to store them. I like keeping apples, bananas, and other fresh items out on the dining room table as an organic centerpiece. One way to stock up on extra containers is to turn old pans and flea market finds into serving pieces. The original purpose of that Bundt pan may have been to bake a cake, but it can just as easily serve a different purpose on your table. Apply some enamel paint and fill it with green apples to reintroduce that Bundt pan to your table. Make a cake plate using a plate and two ramekins, and then glue everything together with superstrong crafter's glue. You can create a lot of clever tableware this way—maybe you'll start making dinner every night just so you can use it.

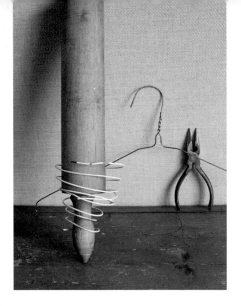

SPRING FLING

You can skip the steak part of this *steak frites*-inspired project. This is a crafty way to make the ubiquitous frites (french fries) serving piece every French bistro uses. Repurpose two wire hangers and fashion them into a spring shape that will sit nicely on your table—you can put breadsticks, strawberries, chips, or fries inside if you like.

Take the wire clothes hangers, snip the hanging hook off with wire snips or pliers. Bend one end of both wire pieces, hooking them together. Wind smaller-gauge wire tightly around the place where you've hooked the wires together. Once you have securely tied the two separate pieces together, you will have a long piece of wire to work with. You can use a wooden rolling pin to help wind the wire. You might need to use the pliers to make the first turn in one end, then wrap the long piece around your rolling pin. After you have a spring-shaped piece, mold it so that it resembles a funnel—

a larger opening at the top with a smaller base at the bottom. Make the base steady by pulling it open a little bit. Next, use spray enamel to paint the vessel, let it dry, and start making more to create a whole table setting. When you're ready to put them to work, take a cloth napkin, roll it into a funnel shape, and place it inside the new vessel. *Et voilà, fait accompli!*

THREE-TIERED TRAY

Here is another way to make use of old plates. This tiered tray makes it easy to serve dessert when you have company for dinner. Cookies, brownies, and other sweet treats can be placed before you sit down. When it's time, all you need to do is grab this tray and put it on the table. Or use this server for appetizers, or fill it with fruit for an edible centerpiece. It even makes a nice presentation of little flower pots. But I think the best use is for some delicious cupcakes.

Tools and Materials
› Safety glasses
› Glass or tile drill bit
› Drill
› 2–3 plates in graduated sizes (such as dinner and salad plates)
› Lamp kit (comes with an electrical-wire threaded lamp rod and matching nuts and washers)
› 1–2 lamp spacers of equal size
› Round lamp finial

How To

1. Put on your stylish safety glasses. Put a glass or tile bit in your drill and drill a hole through the center of each plate. Make the hole the same diameter as the lamp rod.
2. Attach a nut and washer to one end of the lamp rod.
3. Insert the rod through the bottom hole of the bigger plate.
4. Turn the piece right-side up and add a lamp spacer.
5. Attach a washer and nut.
6. Place the smaller plate on the lamp rod.
7. Secure it with another washer and nut. Repeat steps 6 and 7 if using 3 plates.
8. To complete your project, attach the lamp finial. I like an open circle finial because it is the perfect handle with which to carry the tray.

Note: Instead of a lamp kit and spacers, use inverted teacups to separate the tiers. Glue in place with a glue gun.

NAPKIN CHAIR COVER

When I was growing up, I had my own chair at the dining table called "Emily's chair." It was just like everyone else's chair, except for one thing—it was filthy. Apparently, I was a messy eater. To my parents' credit, they still allowed me to sit at the table, and eventually I stopped spilling. At some point, someone had mercy on that chair and put new fabric on the seat. In case you have your own Emily, here's an easy idea for a simple, temporary slipcover: Sew two ribbon ties to each corner of an old cloth napkin. Place the napkin on your chair and tie each corner to a chair leg. *Voilà!*

TRANSFORM A TABLE

Painting isn't the only way to repurpose something destined for the trash. The classic card table may be ugly, but get your hands on one and all you need to do is cover the top with oilcloth fabric (which is great, because you can wipe it down). Use a staple gun to attach the cloth to the underside of the table. You can close up the table and slide it into your closet, then pull it out whenever you need extra room at the table.

Note: This idea works with any table, just be sure you have a strong enough staple gun if you're using a wood table.

FABRIC REMNANT TABLECLOTH

Repurpose extra fabric into a practical tablecloth. Fabric remnants are sold for a discount at fabric stores, which is good way to get really nice material at a steep discount. Fabric samples are also good to get your hands on— most interior designers have more samples than they know what to do with.

ECO-BIT: CLOTH NAPKINS

Each year, each person in the United States uses the equivalent of one Douglas fir tree in paper products. Using recycled paper instead of virgin paper creates 74 percent less air pollution and uses 50 percent less water (source: EPA, 2008). Although cloth napkins still require the use of energy and water to clean, that has a significantly lower impact than paper, even if the paper is recycled.

Find designers who may be interested in getting rid of some of their stash and you could get some nice material for very little money. You can also repurpose curtains into tablecloths; keep this in mind next time you're at a thrift store or flea market. Hemming fabric to use as a tablecloth isn't even necessary. If the fabric fits on your table, you can make it work. I like the raw edges. We tied a piece of waxed twine around our impromptu table-cloth to keep it in place and add a touch of whimsy.

BUTTON NAPKIN RINGS

The switch to cloth napkins can be even more appealing with these sweet napkin rings. Extra buttons can be a really cute—and useful—part of your table setting with just a little ribbon, and another good reason to use cloth napkins. Loop a thin piece of ribbon through the buttonholes, tie the two ribbon ends into a knot, and wrap a folded napkin with it, looping the end around the button to keep it in place.

NATURAL CENTERPIECE

When you plant a kitchen garden outside, of course you will want to plant some flowers, too. Until you have beautiful blooms, you can create a lovely reusable centerpiece without them. I often suggest handmade centerpieces for an event, simply because there are so many unresolved issues with the flower industry (see the following Eco-Bit: "Better Blossoms"). For this project, all you will need are a few branches, a sweater or felt, scissors, buttons, and a cherry blossom stencil. If you can't find a stencil, you can download a paper alternative. For stencils, go to www.stencil-library.com.

ECO-BIT: BETTER BLOSSOMS

The flower industry uses a wide range of chemicals, some with the potential for serious harm to human health. Countries outside of the United States are not held to the same regulations for the use of harmful pesticides. Imported flowers must be pest free, so non-U.S. growers are very liberal in their use of pesticides. And since they are not an edible crop, U.S. inspectors do not test the level of pesticide residues. For a healthier alternative, buy locally grown, in-season blooms.

Tools and Materials

› 1 pink wool sweater (if you don't have pink, you can dye a light-colored sweater the right color), or pieces of felt
› Fabric scissors
› Cherry blossom stencil
› Black felt tip pen
› Craft glue
› 12 or more 1-inch plain black buttons
› Needle and pink thread
› 4 or 5 small branches, about 3 feet long
› Several 1-pound bags of uncooked beans (use any beans—kidney, black-eyed, or garbanzo—or lentils; all are nice shapes and good colors for this project)
› 1 glass vase or other container

How To

1. Machine wash a pink wool sweater in hot water to turn it into felt. Lay the sweater flat to dry (overnight).

2. Once the sweater is dry, place the cherry blossom stencil on the sweater (or felt pieces) and trace around it with the black felt tip pen. You will want to have at least a dozen blossoms.
3. Cut out the traced blossoms.
4. Place a black button in the center of each blossom and glue or sew it in place.
5. Glue each blossom to a different spot on the branches.
6. Fill the vase with beans or lentils to 2 inches below the rim.
7. Slide each branch into the beans and arrange; the beans will hold your beautiful arrangement in place.

Note: The height of a centerpiece should sit below the eye level of someone seated at the table. Though this centerpiece may be tall, there are ways to ensure nobody's vision is blocked: Once you've arranged the piece, sit at each chair to strategically arrange the branches so everyone's gaze is unobstructed.

CLAY CACHEPOT

This project is a way to make any simple clay pot into a vase you can use on your dining room table. Clay pots are inexpensive, and there always seems to be a lot of them hanging around. In addition to using them for planting, they're good for baking, storing, and decorating. I just like having them around; they remind me of my grandmother's beautiful gardens. You can even use them as cachepots for cut flowers.

Tools and Materials
› Wood filler
› Putty knife/paint spatula (1-½ inch)

› Water sealant (Safecoat
  MexeSeal)
› Newspaper
› Enamel spray paint
› Sandpaper
› Rag
› Paintbrush (1 inch)

Note: Before you begin painting, use wood filler to plug the
drainage hole on the bottom of
the pot. Wood filler is a great
material to have around the
house for a multitude of projects from repairing cracks and chips to plugging
holes. If you want to change a cupboard or dresser door pull to a knob, you
can just plug one hole with wood filler. Wood filler comes in different colors
so you can match it to your project. Don't worry about the color here, though,
since we're painting the pots.

How To

1. Plug the pot's drainage hole with wood filler. First, stuff a piece of
   newspaper down into the bottom of the pot. Keep the newspaper out
   of the hole, though, since we're going to fill it. Turn the pot over so the
   hole faces up, and put about 1 tablespoon of wood filler into the hole
   using a scraping motion with the putty knife.
2. Fill the hole, scraping the excess with the putty knife to be sure you
   have a level surface. The filler will dry in about 30 minutes.
3. Sand the bottom of the pot smooth when dry, and continue sanding the
   entire surface area of the pot inside and out to remove any extra dirt
   and give you a clean surface for painting.

4. Use a damp rag to wipe the pot clean once you finish the sanding. If the pot is damp after wiping it down, let it dry before applying the water sealant.

5. Apply the water sealant with a paintbrush so you can use the pot for cut flowers if you'd like. I recommend Safecoat MexeSeal because it is specifically made for clay surfaces, and unlike traditional sealants, it does not contain formaldehyde or other toxic ingredients. It's also nonflammable. All you need is a thin coat of sealant. Let dry.

6. Paint the outside of the pot with enamel spray paint. (I like to stick with a solid color.)

7. When the paint is dry, apply another layer of sealant with your paintbrush to make the cachepot watertight. If you're lucky enough to have a garden like my grandmother's, just go out back and cut some blooms for your new cachepot.

SALT AND PEPPER BUD VASE

Salt and pepper shakers are another nice way to bring flowers to your table. Clean the insides well, add a little water, and your flowers will be sitting pretty. Save the tops as creative place card holders—add a little copper wire through the holes and twist it into a spiral to give place cards a perch to stay put.

BEDROOM
Sleep Tight

Every bedroom has one thing in common—sleep. But besides being the place we lay our heads at night, many bedrooms pull double duty as an office or movie-watching station. When reducing energy, remember that the computer and television require an enormous amount of it. Put electronics on a power strip and turn everything off when not in use. It's not just a healthy planet you should worry about—the bedroom can also make you sick. Traditionally grown cotton and nonorganic sheets can be laden with pesticides and other unidentified toxins. The mattress might not be any better. Do yourself a favor and invest in truly organic cotton bedding that is completely toxin-free. Handmade bedding is a great way to up the health factor when you sleep. This chapter offers ideas that are not only easy and chic but could also help you sleep better.

SWEATER QUILT

This project gives new meaning to the phrase "put a sweater on." I don't know about you, but I heard that uttered with regularity. I grew up in a drafty old house where cold winter nights always included nice warm wool blankets—blankets that kept me warm no matter what. I'm not sure where those blankets came from or where I can get them today (without spending an arm and a leg), but I do know that this project comes pretty close to replicating the warmth and comfort I derived from the wool blankets of my childhood, and it makes a wonderful throw for your bedroom.

Tools and Materials

› 4 wool sweaters (more if your blanket is bigger)
› Fabric scissors
› Newspaper
› Paper scissors
› Fabric pencil or chalk
› Blanket of approximate size you want the sweater quilt to be
› Sewing machine
› 1 yard of 45-inch-wide fabric (use a remnant or repurpose an old top sheet)
› Iron and ironing board
› Straight pins
› Tape measure

How To

1. Machine wash four wool sweaters in hot water and lay flat to dry.
2. Cut off the arms and shoulder and side seams of each sweater so you have one big piece of felt, with the neck hole in the middle.

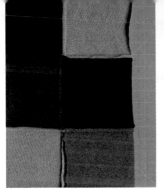

3. Cut a 6-inch-by-6-inch-square template out of newspaper. Lay the template on the sweater, trace around it with the fabric pencil or chalk. Fit as many squares as possible on each sweater. Cut out the squares.

4. Lay out a blanket of the approximate size you want your new wool blanket to be. Place all of the squares in the arrangement you like. (The blanket will help you lay the squares out in an even grid.)

5. Pin the squares together at the edges. The easiest way to put this blanket together is to first sew the squares into rows and then sew each to the next row.

6. Once your blanket is put together, lay it flat on the floor. If you want perfect edges, trim along the sides—the nice thing about felt is that it won't unravel if you cut it.

7. Lay your backing fabric flat. Cut a piece that is 2 inches wider than the felt squares piece.

8. Lay the sweater quilt on top of the backing, with the seam allowance showing on all sides.

9. Fold the top edges of the fabric over (not under) and iron the folds in place.

10. Fold the edges over again to slightly overlap the felt squares.
11. Pin in place and sew all four sides of the blanket.

SHEET DRAPES

Drapes can be expensive, so save money and make your own by repurposing old bed sheets to make new drapes. Pretty much any size flat sheet can be used, but ideally sheets will be the right length and width for the window you want to dress up, since the real beauty in this method is that there's a minimal amount of work. The top edge of the sheet is a perfect place for the curtain rod—just use a seam splitter to open the hem on both sides of the sheet. Add a stitch around the opening to keep the curtain from unraveling, and you're ready to get hanging. With such an easy project, why not add a little flair before you call it curtains? Use fabric paint to create your own hand-painted drapes that match your style perfectly. Vertical stripes are easy and attractive; simply use a paint roller and alternating colors to match your home decor.

ECO-BIT: WINDOW PROTECTION

The amount of energy lost through windows can be cut significantly by adding drapes. In winter you'll keep the heat indoors, and in summer you'll keep the hot sun out.

LADDER CLOTHES RACK

Part of the reason we let our closets get so jumbled is that we may not be able to see everything clearly. This project will create an instant walk-in "closet" to make organizing your clothes really easy. I am always hoping for more space to hang my clothes, and this handy ladder rack is a great solution. You can pull this closet out when you need extra hanging space—or keep it out all of the time. You will need to get your hands on two identical used ladders.

Tools and Materials

›   2 identical wooden ladders (5-feet high)
›   1 wooden closet rod, 6-feet long and 2-inches in diameter (look on treecycle.org, or ask a local contractor—they might have some old closet rods from a project they are working on)
›   2 metal pipe grip ties, 2 inches (match the rod), with matching screws
›   Electric drill
›   Black felt tip pen
›   Medium-size paintbrush
›   Screwdriver
›   Measuring tape
›   2 pints low-VOC paint
›   Drop cloth
›   Sandpaper

›   Rag
›   Hangers

How To
1. Sand the surface area of both ladders to remove dirt and debris.
2. Place the grip ties on top of each ladder in the center of the top step. The ladders should be open, with the steps facing out to the left and right.
3. Mark the placement where the screws will go to attach the grip ties (2 to 4 holes per tie). Put the grip ties to the side.
4. Drill holes for the screws (you will attach the grip ties later).
5. Wipe the ladders clean with a damp rag and allow the wood to dry (about an hour).
6. Paint both ladders using the medium-size paintbrush.
7. Paint the closet rod and the metal grip ties. Allow everything to dry overnight.
8. Place the ladders where you want them to go, steps facing you and directly opposite one another, exactly 3 feet apart.
9. Drill to bolt the grip ties to the top of each ladder, but leave the screws loose until you put the closet rod in each grip tie. Use a screwdriver to tighten the screws.
10. Because this closet doesn't have a door, keep things uniform by using the same type of coat hangers (you can make your own with the Fancy Hanger project also in this chapter).

Note: You could use milkpaint from page 74 instead of the low-VOC paint.

FOLDING SCREEN

Even if you've sorted through your clothes and made a drop-off at Goodwill, you still may have trouble keeping a tidy closet—or maybe you have trouble getting your clothes to the closet at all. No worries, you can give your mess a temporary hiding place with this easy-to-make folding screen. This project entails getting your hands on durable cardboard or scrap wood pieces—you can even repurpose old shutters. A good place to look for cardboard is at the local appliance store; they have a ton of it and I'm sure would be happy to unload some for free. We turned our folding screen into a chalkboard using paint, so now it's a handy message board, too.

Tools and Materials
› 1 pint primer
› 1 pint black chalkboard paint
› 1 pint regular paint
› Paintbrush
› 4 cardboard panels, 5 feet by 2 feet
› Electric drill
› Drill bit (to fit screws for the hinges)
› 6 ¾-inch hinges
› Screws (to fit hinges)
› Felt tip pan

How To
1. Lay the panels side by side, lined up at the top and bottom. Wipe them clean with a damp cloth.
2. Put each of the hinges, opened, 6 inches from the top of the panels and 6 inches from the bottom.

3. Mark with the pen where the screws for the hinges will go. Put the hinges to the side.
4. Drill holes where the pen marks are.
5. Paint the entire surface area of each panel with a layer of primer. Let doors dry overnight.
6. Apply primer to the other side of the panels. Let dry overnight.
7. Paint one side of doors with the chalkboard paint. Dry for 48 hours.
8. Paint the opposite side of panels. Dry for 48 hours.
9. Attach the hinges, and put your new screen in place. It's best to keep the screen on hardwood floors or some other noncarpeted flooring.

ECO-BIT: NATURAL BRIGHTENING

After a few washes, clothes can become a little dingy. This is because soap builds up and gets trapped in the fabric. Bleach is one solution for lighter colors, but bleach is a highly toxic substance that can take centuries to decompose. There are better eco-options available when it comes to buying bleach, but the best thing to do is to avoid using it at all. As an alternative, try letting the sun do the whitening for you. Add one-half cup of lemon juice to your wash and hang it up to dry outside. When mixed with the heat of the sun, the lemon juice acts as a natural bleach.

FANCY HANGERS

Dry cleaners are happy to get wire hangers back from customers, but you can reuse them yourself with this project. These hangers will also look nice on your ladder closet, and give you incentive to hang your clothes up. Taking care of your clothes is just one more way to make your things last longer, and thereby reduce your consumption. Plus, remaking ugly wire hangers means you don't have to spend money on the non-eco-friendly plastic ones.

Tools and Materials
› Several men's cotton shirts (use the leftover fabric from the Hanging Organizer project in the chapter titled "Entryway")
› Fabric scissors
› Fabric pen or chalk
› Sewing needle
› Thread
› Wire hangers
› Grosgrain ribbon
› Fabric glue

How To
1. Cut four 2-inch-wide strips of fabric.
2. Take a wire hanger and one strip of fabric. Place a dot of glue on one end of the fabric, and beginning at the tip of the hanger handle, wind it tightly around the tip of the hanger twice.
3. Wrap the whole handle by winding the fabric, overlapping each time you wind it around the handle. Keep winding the fabric around the entire hanger.

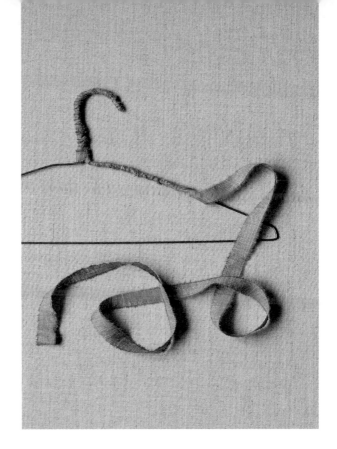

4. When you reach the end of the first fabric piece, glue the end to the wire.

5. Take another piece, glue the end of it to where you left off.

6. Continue winding the fabric until you get back to the base of the handle.

7. Place a dot of glue on the end of the piece, and wind it around to finish. For a little added charm, use about 6 inches of grosgrain ribbon to tie a bow at the base of the handle.

DRESSER DRAWER STORAGE

When you're in search of extra storage, or maybe doing a quick cleanup job, you may be tempted to stash things under the bed. This is fine so long as you do it in a way that won't create a dust bunny haven. Take advantage of that space and keep things easy to clean with this project. These drawers will give you extra storage that's accessible, and you won't end up with a dusty black hole under your bed. Directions are for one drawer, but you can make as many as will fit under the bed.

Tools and Materials
› 4 square wood pieces (each piece should be about 4-inches wide and 2-inches thick)
› 4 flush-mount casters
› 1 dresser drawer that will fit under your bed with at least 4 inches of height to spare
› Electric drill
› Sewing machine
› 1 yard of canvas, or enough to cover the top of your drawer with a 2-inch seam allowance all the way around
› 4 strips of Velcro, the same length as the drawer
› Wood glue

How To
1. Drill a hole in the middle of each of four wood squares for a caster.
2. Glue a wood square to each of the bottom corners of the drawer.
3. Attach the casters to the drawer.

4. Hem each edge of a canvas piece.
5. Sew the looped side of Velcro strips to both side edges of the canvas piece.
6. Attach the grip side of Velcro to the tops of the sides of the drawer.
7. Place the fabric covers on the drawers, fill them with items to be stored, and roll them under your bed.

Note: Find old dresser drawers at flea markets or thrift stores. Or you can take the drawers out of an old dresser and use the Dressed-up Cabinet project in this chapter to repurpose the rest of it.

LAVENDER SACHETS

Just when you start getting used to the cold weather, it's time to put your winter things away. If you store them carefully, they will last you many seasons. That means making sure moths don't dine on the wool while it's in storage. I don't know about you, but finding a moth hole in a favorite sweater is totally depressing. Moth balls aren't the answer—they're made from chemical pesticides and deodorant. Forget the mothballs and switch to the sweet-smelling alternative of lavender. Cedar chips, cedar oil, and rosemary work, too. Make sachets by sewing pieces of fabric together on three sides, fill fabric with dried lavender, and stitch the open edge closed. Place the sachets in your drawers and closets and you'll have protected clothes that smell sweet, too. The fabric you choose should have a very fine weave, such as the organza shirt I repurposed, so the scent is released.

ECO-BIT: GREEN DRY CLEANING

We only occasionally use the dry cleaner, sometimes for my husband's shirts or sweaters. When we do have something cleaned, we use "green" cleaners. These are dry cleaners that have made the switch from the petroleum-based cleaning solution known as perc (perchloroethylene). Perc was the first chemical to be classified as a carcinogen by the Consumer Product Safety Commission. The Environmental Protection Agency lists perc as a neurotoxin and an eye and skin irritant. Find local cleaners who instead use the carbon dioxide cleaning process.

GARMENT BAG

Storing clothes in cloth is healthier and better for the clothes than storing them in plastic. When something is kept in a closed plastic container or bag, chemicals from the plastic are released, creating a toxic environment that wears down the fibers. To make a simple cloth garment bag, sew two old pillowcases together. Turn both pillowcases inside out. Cut the bottom off of one pillowcase so it has two open ends. Sew the open edge of the second pillowcase to the raw edge of the first pillowcase. Cut a small opening in the top pillowcase for the hangers to stick out. Stitch around the edge to finish the hanger opening. Lay the piece flat. Place a hanger where it would be once you have the finished piece. Use a ruler to draw a line on the left and right corners, along the top sides of the hanger. Remove both corners with scissors. Sew both corners closed and turn your new garment bag right-side out. Take a few of these to the dry cleaner next time you make a drop-off and ask that they use your cloth garment bags in lieu of the plastic usually used.

HANDMADE HANDKERCHIEF

Take the same fabric that you used to make the sachets to make a few nice cloth handkerchiefs. This item is a relic from a bygone era that's ready for a comeback. You may think it's not very hygienic to reuse the same thing again and again, so you should have more than one on hand, that's for sure. Switching from paper tissues is more than just a good eco-decision—personal care paper products are often made with chemicals such as petroleum and silicon that are harmful to humans and to our environment. All you need to make a handkerchief (or a few) is an old article of clothing, preferably something soft like brushed cotton. Lay the shirt, skirt, or whatever you have flat on a cutting surface. Use a straight edge and measuring tape to draw an 8-inch-by-8-inch square. Cut out the square with fabric scissors. Fold one side, iron it flat, then fold again, iron it flat. Pin that side in place, and repeat on all sides. Sew a finished hem all the way around. Now fold it up nicely and you can look forward to your next sneeze.

ECO-BIT: SILENT SPRING

DDT was once a widely used pesticide that is now banned by the World Health Organization. The ban was in response to the unchecked use of pesticides and their effect on living organisms, which Rachael Carson wrote about in her seminal work *Silent Spring* in 1962.

DRESSED-UP CABINET

Don't get rid of the dresser you may have used in the Dresser Drawer Storage project, you'll need it for this project. When dresser drawer runners get broken, opening and closing them can be frustrating. Or if they aren't securely in place, they can fall out and land on your foot. You can fix the runners, or you can repurpose the dresser into a storage cabinet. An old dresser without the drawers can make a great cabinet that works in any room of your house. Remove all of the interior parts with a handheld electric saw (wear protective eyewear and work gloves). Use a rasp to sand the entire inside smooth. If you want, add a coat of paint or put up wallpaper. The cabinet can be left open with a neat pile of quilts inside, or stack boxes, towels, almost anything. You could even put a couple of shelves inside to make a bookshelf. If you want to hide the items away, make a little curtain for the cabinet by placing a tension curtain rod and a piece of fabric across the front.

LIGHTING
Bright Ideas

Repurposing materials in creative ways has many different benefits, including reducing our energy footprint. By reusing something, we reduce the amount of waste we produce and save the energy that would have been used to create something new. The definition of energy as a concept is somewhat transitory. In today's world, energy is most often created from fossil fuels that are then used for power, including the light in our homes. There are cleaner ways of producing power, but until these become the norm, we must be more aggressive in reducing energy use. Reevaluating how much light we use in the home is a critical step in this process. The fact is, often we use too much light in areas that do not require it.

To begin, design a lighting plan for your home to identify where you need light, and what type of light you need in the different areas of living space. This chapter is made up of lighting projects to help you prioritize the amount of light you use. There are three main categories of interior lighting: ambient, which provides a soft glow to a room; accent lighting, which puts light in a specific spot to give attention to an area or object; and task lighting, which is meant to be used, as you've probably guessed, for specific tasks like reading, cooking, needlework, and so on. Natural light and artificial light can work together in an energy-efficient plan, and your lighting fixtures are a key element of that plan.

HANDMADE LAMP

The height of a lamp, the type of shade, and even the shape of a lamp itself all contribute to the quality of light it provides. Making your own lamp gives you the freedom to choose what type of light you want from it— maybe you need a lamp for an entryway, in which case a smaller size might be in order. Or perhaps you'd like to have fewer lamps in your living room— make one or two that will provide better light, thereby reducing the energy you use. Once you see how easy it is to make your own lamp, you'll wonder why you ever spent money buying new ones. No one understood lamp design better than my grandmother Lucille. She always made the lamps in her home, and she had the ability to make them both beautiful and efficient. I still have one of her lamps in my daughter's room, and it shines just the right amount of light for her to play and read by.

Tools and Materials

› 2 matching clay pots
› 1 lamp kit (see Note on page 147), rod should be only 2 inches higher than the two pots stacked
› 2 cups dried lentil beans
› 12-inch-by-12-inch cotton or lightweight canvas fabric
› Sewing machine
› CFL lightbulb
› Felt coaster (see page 72)
› Porcelain paint
› Small (2-inch wide) paintbrush
› Craft glue

ECO-BIT: SOLAR AND DAYLIGHTING
Natural light, obviously, is the light the sun provides. There are newer technologies that can capture daylight, store it, and let you use it even when the sun goes down. Solar panels capture the sun's energy and feed that into the home as power. Daylighting systems also capture the sun's light, but their technology actually feeds the sunlight into an interior space— allowing people to light entire rooms naturally.

How To

1. Paint both pots with porcelain paint and allow to dry.
2. Make a little bean bag to fit in the bottom pot—this will create a steady base as well as provide support for the lamp rod. Cut out two matching pieces of fabric. Our bean bag was about 4 inches by 2 inches, but you can make the bag larger or smaller depending on the size of your pots.
3. Sew three sides together, leaving the top open. Fill with beans, leaving a little room so you can mold the bag to fit perfectly inside the bottom pot. Sew the top side closed.
4. Take the felt coaster, fold in half and cut a hole roughly 2 inches wide in the center of the coaster—this is where the lamp cord will feed through. Glue the felt piece to the underside of the bottom pot, making sure to center the hole in the coaster with the hole in the bottom of the pot. Trim the excess from around the edge of the pot so the felt is hidden.
5. Fit the bean bag into the bottom pot, base surface down. Feed the lamp cord through the pot, pulling it through the bottom hole and felt piece.
6. Set the pot down, fit the lamp rod into the base and mold the bean bag around for stability. You are checking to make sure that the lamp rod fits comfortably in the base. Remove the lamp rod and set aside.
7. Place glue all the way around the rim of the bottom pot and place the top pot rim to rim with the bottom pot. Hold with firm pressure for a few seconds then allow to dry.
8. Once the glue has dried, slide the lamp rod down through the hole of the top pot and out the hole in the bottom pot, leaving just enough rod sticking out to secure with one lug nut at the bottom. Then feed

the cord (non-plug side) up through the bottom of the rod, pulling it out of the top of the rod, leaving about 2 inches of cord extending beyond the rod's top.

9. Attach the second lug nut to the rod's top, screwing it down so it is flush with the pot, but not so tight that you crack the terracotta.

10. Attach the "neck" to the top of the rod, making sure it fits just inside the hole. Follow the manufacturer's instructions to assemble the rest of your lamp kit.

Note: A lamp kit should include:

› Lamp rod
› Finnial
› Harp
› Electric cord
› Neck (You may have to buy this separately. The circumference should be slightly smaller than the hole in the pot.)

A good lamp kit resource is www.nationalartcraft.com. They sell many lamp kits and extra parts and provide great lamp-making tips.

ECO-BIT: NATURAL ENERGY

By harnessing wind, sunlight, plant matter, or heat from the earth's core, we can produce electricity that is environmentally friendly. Individuals can reduce the amount of electricity they use in myriad ways, such as installing storm doors and windows and keeping the thermostat at 68 degrees F in winter and 73 degrees F in summer.

LIGHT READING

This project is a chic way to provide task lighting practically anywhere you want it. You can easily convert a simple hardware lamp into a clip lamp perfect for bedtime reading. All you need is enamel spray paint, a wrench, a rubber clamp (available at the hardware store), and a metal T-bolt clamp (try www.fastfittings.com). You can clip this light onto practically anything—a table, bookshelf, or windowsill. You can also take it outside to your deck or patio if you need a little extra illumination. Just apply a coat or two of paint to the outside of the lamp and let it dry overnight. Then attach the rubber clamp to the lamp base with the T-bolt clamp.

REMADE SHADE

The color of a lampshade makes all the difference because it controls the amount of light you get—the lighter the shade, the more light it allows. On the other hand, worn or faded shades can make a room feel drab. Brighten up your room by replacing the fabric or paper of an old dark lampshade with a lighter color. This is a pretty easy (and inexpensive) skill to master; once you get the technique down, you'll be amazed at how much fun it is to renew lampshades.

Tools and Materials
› Old lampshade
› Large sheet of craft paper
› Pencil
› Paper scissors
› Fabric large enough to amply cover shade (remember that the darker the fabric, the less light will shine through)

> Fabric pencil or chalk
> Fabric scissors
> Hot glue gun and glue sticks
> 1 yard of grosgrain ribbon
> Clothespins

How To

1. Place a lampshade on its side with the seam on one edge of a sheet of craft paper (large enough to fit around the lamp shade, with a couple of extra inches at the top and bottom).
2. Roll the shade along the paper, using pencil to mark the top and bottom edges of the shade on the paper as you go. When you get back to the seam (where you started), you will have a flat outline of the shade on the paper. This is your template.
3. Add 1 inch on all sides of the outline and cut out the template.
4. Place the shade template on top of the fabric and trace around it with a fabric pencil or chalk, drawing the template shape on the fabric piece.
5. Cut the template shape out of the fabric. Test fit the fabric on the shade and trim the fabric if necessary.
6. Lay the fabric piece wrong-side up and line up the seam on the lamp shade with one edge of the fabric template.
7. Apply a strip of hot glue to the fabric edge and lay the seam of the shade on top, pressing lightly to adhere to the glue.
8. Start rolling the shade along the fabric, applying glue to the fabric where the shade connects to it.
9. Periodically smooth the fabric against the shade, getting rid of any bumps or bubbles and making sure the shade and fabric fit together tightly. Use clothespins to help hold the fabric in place.

10. After the glue has dried a bit, trim the excess fabric with small scissors.
11. Measure the diameter of the top and bottom of the shade and cut four pieces of ribbon trim (two for top, two for bottom).
12. Glue a piece of trim to the outside of the top and bottom of the shade.
13. Repeat on the inside of the shade—gluing the pieces of trim to the top and bottom—to cover the raw edges of the fabric.
14. Allow to dry, and then put the shade in place.

BOOKSHELF LIGHT

Indirect lighting can reduce energy use because we prioritize where we really need direct lighting, then use alternative lighting where we don't need as much. Bookshelves are one example of where you can use indirect lighting. Adding a bookshelf light is a nice way to brighten things up. This project adds light to an area that may not need much and is a unique way to repurpose nonrecyclable CD jewel cases.

Tools and Materials
› 5 identical CD jewel cases
› 1 yard eyelet material
› Fabric pencil or chalk
› Fabric scissors
› Spray adhesive
› Glue gun and glue sticks
› Adhesive craft tape (2 inches wide, silver or white)
› Preassembled small lamp kit (available at most hardware stores)

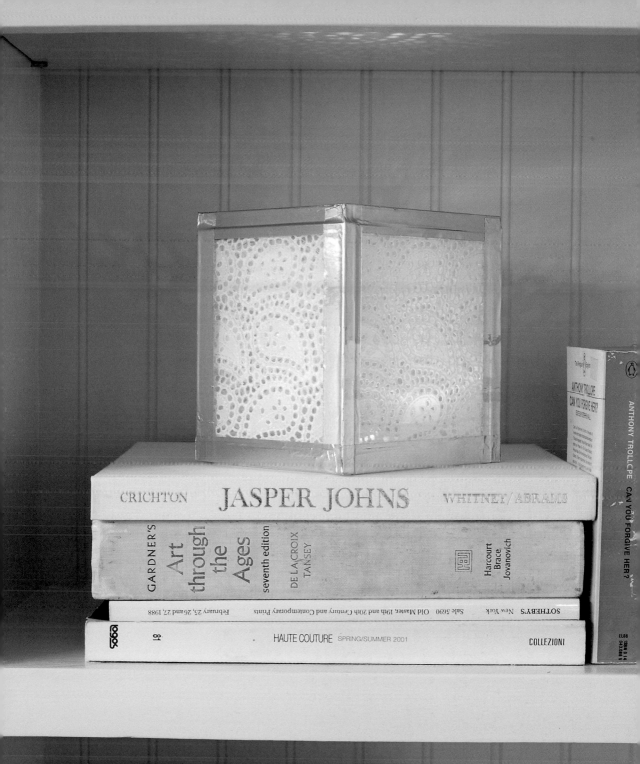

CRICHTON   JASPER JOHNS   WHITNEY/ABRAMS

GARDNER'S Art through the Ages seventh edition DE LA CROIX TANSEY   Harcourt Brace Jovanovich

SOTHEBY'S New York Sale 5690 Old Master, 19th and 20th Century and Contemporary Prints February 25, 26 and 27, 1988

COLLEZIONI HAUTE COUTURE SPRING/SUMMER 2001 81 1990s

ANTHONY TROLLOPE CAN YOU FORGIVE HER?

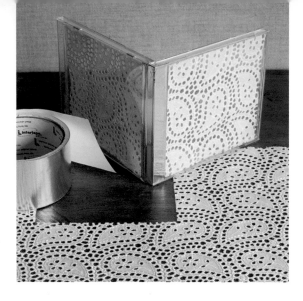

How To

1. Remove the paper inserts from inside the cases, front and back. You'll have to pull out the tray piece that holds the CD in the case. Once you've taken the back cover out, replace the tray.
2. Lay out the eyelet and use a fabric pencil or chalk to trace around one of the inserts, five times. These pieces of fabric will line the cases.
3. Open the five cases so they lay flat.
4. Apply spray adhesive to the inside of the first case, then place the eyelet inside. Repeat this step with the four other cases.
5. To assemble the sides of the light box, begin with two closed cases, placing them together at a right angle with the opening part of the CD case facing out, the hinge at the top.
6. Use a piece of tape to attach the two cases to each other.
7. Use a second piece of tape to attach the cases along the edge, on the inside. Repeat this with the next two cases.
8. Place the last case on the top, and neatly adhere tape along the edges.
9. Stick the lamp underneath the new box light, and place it on your bookshelf with the cord feeding out the back.

STRING OF LIGHTS

A string of LED lights uses a very small amount of energy and adds just the right amount of light for an outdoor soiree. Add a little sparkle to your outdoor entertaining space with this project. You will also be repurposing something we have plenty of—egg cartons. You'll need three cardboard egg cartons, so start saving up your farm fresh, organic egg containers. When you have enough, just trim the twelve egg "cups" out of each carton. Poke a hole in the bottom of each cup with an awl. Take your strand of LED lights and push a bulb through the center of each paper cup. Make sure the paper is sitting on the socket, not on the bulb. The LED lights shouldn't get hot enough to be a fire hazard, but don't leave the lights on for too long at one time. Take the garland out for your next backyard party, hang it up, and enjoy your DIY light display.

ECO-BIT: ZERO FOOTPRINT
Zero-footprint homes use renewable energy devices to completely neutralize the impact their energy use has on the planet.

LUMINARIES

If you really want to save energy, turn off the outdoor lights and light the way with these luminaries instead. This is an economical and eco-friendly way to decorate for a party or just add charm to your backyard. Aluminum is easily recyclable, but reusing it in your home is even better. Soup cans with the labels cleaned off make durable and festive outdoor lights. All you need is a metal punch tool (an awl or a screw punch) to create a pattern on the cans for light to come through. Make a hanging handle with jewelry wire, place a small candle inside, and then hang them from a tree, trellis,

ECO-BIT: CHOOSING THE RIGHT LIGHT BULB

Hopefully you have already switched out your old light bulbs in favor of the more energy-efficient variety. I've had trouble figuring out which bulb is for what, so I put together this rundown.

CFL (compact fluorescent light): These are the optimal alternative to incandescent bulbs. CFLs work best to cast light over a short distance. CFLs can be used for table and floor lamps (warm white), reading and task lamps (daylight or warm white), sconces (warm white if shade is gold-toned), and recessed fixtures (warm white). When you're not sure which light bulb you need, you are usually safe with a warm-white CFL, 3,000 degrees Kelvin or lower. They have the color quality most associated with traditional bulbs. To find the approximate CFL equivalent of a traditional bulb, divide the wattage of the traditional bulb by four.

LED (light emitting diode): LEDs are quite expensive compared with the standard incandescent bulbs. However, they last up to ten times longer than incandescent bulbs, which means a cost savings over time. LEDs are ideal for lighting options such as sturdy outdoor fixtures or holiday lights.

Halogen, xenon, or krypton: These are great for indirect lighting, or what I call showcase lighting, such as what you might have in an entrance hall. Fixtures such as chandeliers and pendant lights work well with these bulbs. For the equivalent of an incandescent bulb in halogen, krypton, or xenon, divide the wattage of the traditional bulb by one and a half.

Note: We know that we should move on from using incandescent lights because of the incredible energy loss from just one bulb. I understand why some people prefer the light they give off; after all, lighting as we know it was designed with these bulbs in mind. But there are alternatives that emulate the appearance of incandescent bulbs, including cases to cover the tubing of an energy-efficient bulb, leaving us with no reason not to switch.

or your porch. These also make nice walkway lights to welcome friends out of the dark night. If you don't have something to hang them on, such as a fence, just put a little sand in the bottom to hold the candles and place them on a flat surface.

CANDLESTICK COTERIE

Another way to add energy-free lighting to your home is by grouping different candlesticks together, turning random candlesticks into a dramatic set. Bring cohesion to the coterie with a little paint. A single paint color on each piece of a jumbled assortment will make different candlesticks look like a set. Remake candlesticks you already own or go to the local thrift store and repurpose someone else's cast-offs. Clean the surface of the candlestick with soap and water. Prep for paint by going over the entire surface area with steel wool or sandpaper. Rinse dust and debris off completely with water. Once the candlestick is dry, apply a coat of primer (spray paint is the easiest) over the entire surface, starting at the top of the candlestick. Let the primer dry completely. When the primer is dry, spray on a coat of metallic paint. I like silver or gold metallic, for obvious reasons. For a little extra sparkle, add a fine glitter finish. Simply use spray adhesive, dust the

ECO-BIT: SOLAR CHARGERS

New solar technology seems to come on the market daily and at affordable prices. Everything from solar-panel backpacks that can power a laptop to solar cars to solar bikes for the really lazy are available. For about twenty dollars you can find solar-powered strings of LED lights, which makes your outdoor lighting hands- and energy-free.

candlesticks with the glitter, and shake lightly to remove the excess. Let the candlesticks dry overnight. After about a day, everything should be completely dry and you can feel free to light up.

TEACUP CANDLES

Try this simple candle project to give your orphaned teacups a makeover. These little teacup candles can be used anywhere in your home. Besides giving you another option to reduce your energy consumption, this is an opportunity to keep burned candles from going in the trash by melting them down for a new candle.

Take used beeswax or soy candles, melt them down in a pot on the stove using a low heat seating. Place a metal-ended wick in the cup (available from candle supply stores or craft stores), wrap the end of the wick around a pencil, leaving enough wick so that the metal end sits directly on the bottom of the cup. There should be no slack in the wick. Balance the pencil across the lip of the cup. Pour the melted wax into the cup, filling it to within an inch of the top. Wait for the wax to harden. Remove the pencil and trim the wick to about one-half inch.

DELIGHTFUL MATCHES

For your pretty new candle displays, remake your matches so they too are display-worthy. Keep them right by the candles and you will never have to search your drawers for a match again. Take some used greeting cards, trace an outline on the card around your box of matches (you can use the small kind, or a bigger matchbox). Cut out the template you drew on the card with paper scissors. Put dots of glue on top of the match box, and place the card on top, pressing firmly. Don't cover the flint strip, or you won't be able to use the matches!

LOUNGE LIGHT

Take two extra lampshades that may not have a home and put them to work as indirect lighting for any dark corner of your home. This creative reuse of shades reminds me of a Moroccan lounge. The two shades must match up with each other in diameter on at least one end (top or bottom).

To make, place one shade on top of the other shade, matching sides together. Use embroidery thread and an embroidery needle to sew the shades together. To add some light to the lamp, get a simple hanging lamp kit at the hardware store for a few dollars. Feed the bulb down through the top of the lamp and secure it in place with two pieces of jewelry wire. Insert a hook into the ceiling and attach the cord to the hook. Add a tassel to the bottom to give the lamp an exotic finish. I like this project as a way to camouflage an ugly ceiling light, or even a cool way to add some light to an outdoor affair.

ECO-BIT: USE SOY AND BEESWAX CANDLES

Most candles are made of paraffin wax, a petroleum byproduct. Not only is this an eco faux pas, but it's bad for your health. Paraffin candles emit eleven toxins documented by the American Lung Association, two of which are known carcinogens—toluene and benzene. Soy and beeswax candles are nontoxic and perform as well as the paraffin variety.

HOLIDAYS AND GIFT GIVING
Bring Joy

When we talk about waste, it's impossible not to bring up the holidays. So much waste is produced in such a short amount of time: Between Thanksgiving and New Year's Day, the amount of waste produced by Americans increases by 25 percent (sources: www.use-less-stuff.com, *42 Ways to Trim Your Holiday Waste*). I know this is a bummer to think about when you really just want to enjoy the festivities, but if you take the eco-chic approach, you can still have fun and reduce waste, too.

For one thing, you can request unwrapped gifts. Make an effort to give things that do not have excessive packaging. Buying used items online is one great way to do this. You can also give reusable alternatives (see more ideas throughout this chapter). When you do wrap, rethink wrapping paper. Maybe you can make the wrapping part of the gift, such as a cloth handkerchief (like the one in the chapter titled "Bedroom"). Simplifying gift giving and how you celebrate holidays is easier for you and easier on the environment. This chapter is filled with sophisticated and thoughtful alternatives you can adopt as your own.

GREEN GIFT WRAP

You can stop buying wrapping supplies now—a stash of fabric remnants or old articles of clothing can be made into simple little gift bags in any size. Or make the wrapping part of the gift—like a handmade organic cotton handkerchief. You can also repurpose clothes by using fabric this way. For this project, I recommend sticking to either cotton, wool, or linen fabrics because they are easier to work with. Here's how you can make several gift bags out of one item of clothing.

You'll need a sewing machine, sewing scissors, cutting board, rotary cutter, fabric pen or chalk, seam splitter, measuring tape, flat edge, and an article of clothing such as a wool, cotton, or linen skirt. Lay your piece of material down on a flat surface. Measure the size of the item you plan to put in the gift bag: You'll want the bag to be 2 inches larger on both sides. Add 4 inches to the height so you have room to tie the ribbon. Don't forget to add inches based on the width of the item. Use the ruler to draw a rectangle on the fabric. Cut the two equal size pieces of fabric. Sew a half-inch finished hem on all sides of both pieces. Line the two fabric pieces up with each other so the hem sides face out,

ECO-BIT: FORESTRY STEWARDSHIP COUNCIL

The FSC was created in 1992 in response to a global reaction to depleted resources faced by cultures across the world. It is a worldwide organization made up of interested parties from all aspects of forestry—loggers, environmentalists, foresters, printers. The FSC now has a certification program that acknowledges corporations and their products that are made in a well-managed, renewable forest environment.

pin both together on three sides (the two longer sides, and one shorter side). Turn the piece inside out and sew three sides. Turn the bag right-side out. Take the length of ribbon, put your gift in the bag, and tie the gift bag closed.

ECO-BIT: WRAPPING PAPER

Cheap drugstore wrapping paper often isn't Forest Stewardship Council certified or recyclable. And it's a needless waste of paper when you can usually do a lovely wrapping job with materials you already have. Even newspaper can help to create a perfect package, as long as you dress up the package in other ways. For example, really good ribbon can make it look instantly chic. Build your supply of ribbons, pretty paper, and tissue-paper wrapping items like I do whenever gifts are received. Christmas in particular can provide you with a bonanza of wrapping supplies. I always save the good stuff and reuse it throughout the year.

HANDMADE BOWS

Instead of buying ribbons, make your own out of plastic bags. This project will provide plenty of bows to get you through the holidays. You'll need four plastic grocery bags and a pair of scissors. Directions are for one bow. To begin, cut off the handles of the grocery bags and set them aside. Cut the bags in half by cutting around the sides and bottom of each bag. You now have eight squares of plastic fabric. Cut each square into 2-inch-wide strips. Tie one of the bag handles around the center of the stack, making a knot (or use twine as we did). Fold the stack in half with the knot in the center. Tie another handle around the folded stack, about a half-inch inch above the first tie.

Fluff out the strips and trim to desired size. You should be able to attach the bow to the package with a little tape, or, if you're wrapping with fabric, just attach with a medium safety pin.

TINY PAPER TREES

You might not want to forgo your Christmas tree, but you can reduce in other ways. These trees may be tiny, but they are still a sweet and simple way to repurpose newspaper, aluminum foil, and even computer paper. This project is just another way to dress up your home for the holidays without spending a dime or wasting a resource. You might even consider these as gifts: They're so delicate, you don't need to wrap them to give them. These directions are for one tree only.

Tools and Materials

› 1 or 2 pipe cleaners, depending on desired height (white or silver, but other colors will work too)

- › Newspaper (used decorative paper or gift wrap would also be nice)
- › Used aluminum foil (it's easy to clean in the sink, and the more crinkled, the better)
- › Thin cardboard (a shoe box is perfect)
- › Paper scissors
- › 12-inch ruler
- › X-Acto knife
- › Cutting mat
- › Felt tip pen
- › Japanese paper punch or wooden dowel
- › Pencil
- › ½-inch size bead, with a hole big enough to fit over the pipe cleaner
- › Scrap piece of ribbon

How To

1. Lay paper flat on the cutting mat and use the ruler and felt tip pen to draw *five* squares of *each* size:
   - › ½ by ½ inch
   - › 1 by 1 inch
   - › 1 ½ by 1 ½ inches

> › 2 by 2 inches
> › 2 ½ by 2 ½ inches
> › 3 by 3 inches
> › 3 ½ by 3 ½ inches
> › 4 by 4 inches
> › 4 ½ by 4 ½ inches
> › 5 by 5 inches

2. Cut out each square with an inch between where you cut and the line of the square outline you drew on each piece. You will trim the pieces later.

3. Repeat steps 1 and 2 with the aluminum foil.

4. Stack the newspaper with corresponding sizes of aluminum foil on your cutting mat.

5. Use the ruler and X-Acto knife to trim each size stack neatly, making sure you remove the line made by the felt tip pen in your earlier cut.

6. Cut out a 5-inch-square piece of cardboard; trim it so the sides are clean.

7. With each stack, use the ruler to draw a crisscross from corner to corner very lightly with the pencil, so there is a center point on each stack.

8. Make a tiny hole in the center of each stack with the Japanese paper punch, as well as on the piece of cardboard.

9. Take the pipe cleaner and wind the bottom into a ½-dollar size circle; you can wind it around your finger twice and then make the circle bigger. Bend the pipe cleaner so the circle becomes the bottom, with the center piece extending up (like a tree).

10. Place the bead on the pipe cleaner first (this will weigh it down and keep it from tipping over).

11. Stick the piece of cardboard on next, pulling the pipe cleaner through the center hole so it is flush with the bead. If the cardboard has print, put it on so that the plain cardboard side faces up.

12. Build the rest of your tree with the pieces of paper and aluminum foil: Start with the biggest pieces first, alternating between newspaper and foil. Begin with paper so that you end up with foil as the last piece. When you place the foil, keep the shiny side up. Keep a little distance between each new piece, about one-eighth of an inch. When you place the top piece, trim the pipe cleaner so that there is about 1 inch left above the last piece of foil.
13. Make a tiny bow with the ribbon and affix it to the very top of the tree. Bend the tip of the pipe cleaner over the bow to secure it in place.
14. To store, push all of the paper pieces stacked together at the bottom of your tree, bend the long part so you have a flat piece, and just put it in an envelope for safekeeping.

KEEPSAKE BOX

This project is another way to repurpose old greeting cards. Use your own, or buy a bunch at the next flea market you go to—I've found some amazing ones this way. This box project works with a stiffer paper, which is why greeting cards are a great material to use. These little boxes are so charming that they make a sweet gift all by themselves. Or you can write a tiny note and put it inside. They're an ideal token for those people on your list you want to give a little something to—candy, hair clips, stamps, or jewelry are all items that would be a perfect fit. The easiest way to do this is to use a small cardboard jewelry box as your template.

Tools and Materials
›   1 small used gift box (jewelry sized)
›   Pencil or pen
›   2 used greeting cards

- › Paper scissors
- › X-Acto knife
- › Metal ruler
- › Bone folder
- › Satin or velvet fabric pieces
- › Crafters glue
- › Iron and ironing board
- › Velvet ribbon

How To

1. Carefully take the box bottom apart at the seams (you can use your scissors for this).
2. Lay the disassembled box flat on one greeting card. Decide which part of the greeting card you wish to have showing on the outside of your box. It might even be nice to have some of the handwritten message.
3. Trace the box outline onto a greeting card.
4. Disassemble the top of the box as you did with the bottom, and trace the outline onto the greeting card.
5. Set a metal ruler on one of the folding lines and firmly run a bone folder along the ruler edge. Repeat until each folding line is scored.
6. Trace outlines of your new box top and bottom on a piece of fabric.
7. Assemble the box bottom by folding the sides and using tape inside each corner. Assemble the box top the same way.
8. Apply crafters glue on one side of the fabric, then place it inside your newly assembled box. It should match up so that you don't see the corner seams. Repeat with the fabric for the box top.
9. Allow glue to dry before you put the top onto the new box.
10. Use a small dot of glue to add a pretty velvet ribbon bow to the box top.

POSTCARD GREETINGS

Americans send seven billion greeting cards a year. Greeting cards became all the rage with the introduction of the postage stamp in 1840. Not too many years later, my grandmother and her friends began sending cards to one another. Over the course of their lives, they must have sent hundreds of cards chronicling their life events—births, deaths, and everything in between. Bear in mind that all of my grandmother's friends lived in the same small town she lived in. Thus, greeting cards aren't about reaching out over a long-distance—they're simply about reaching out, whether it's across the country or across the street. You cannot deny the universal appeal of greeting cards, especially since there are now so many printed on recycled paper. To reuse a greeting card, cut off the front (with the picture or design) and use it as a postcard.

ECO-BIT: GREEN GREETINGS

Maybe you are perplexed as to why everyone doesn't just start making recycled paper for everything. Well, unlike glass, which can be recycled forever, paper has a finite lifespan and loses its integrity with each recycling process. This is why you see cards that are "50 percent recycled content."

RE-COVERED DATEBOOK

Obviously we waste paper all year long, not just during the holidays. This project lets you turn something quite wasteful—the promotional vinyl datebook, given out by many companies—into something useful. I worked at a job where I had to order promotional products like pens, paper, notecards, and cups. It's a marketing technique that is way past its prime. Whenever

I see something like this, all I think of is what a terrible waste of resources it is. In this age of eco-awareness, useless promotional items actually do the exact opposite of what is intended—they communicate a negative message, not to mention being way out of date. Speaking of date, the common vinyl personalized datebooks are something I never use but I inevitably end up with at least one every year. Instead of throwing them in the garbage (vinyl can't be recycled), use this project to remake them into something you might want to use or even give as a gift. We are using the rest of the shirt fabric from the Hanging Organizer project in the chapter titled "Entryway," but you can use your own choice of used fabric.

Tools and materials

› 1 yard of fabric
› 24-inch by 12-inch (or larger) piece of used wrapping paper or craft paper (this will go on the inside of the datebook cover)
› Vinyl or other extra datebook, any size will work
› Fabric pencil or chalk
› Black felt tip pen
› Scissors
› Crafters glue
› Bone folder
› Thin piece of cardboard, big enough to cover the datebook (try an empty cereal box)
› Iron and ironing board
› X-Acto knife
› Sewing machine
› Ruler

How To

1. Lay the fabric flat on your cutting surface.
2. Place the datebook open, cover down. Using a straight edge, trace its outline, adding 2 inches all the way around.
3. Hem all four sides of the fabric piece: Fold over each edge, iron it down, then fold again, ironing it down. Sew a finished hem all the way around the fabric piece.
4. Putting the fabric to the side, lay the flat piece of cardboard on your cutting surface, then place the datebook, open, on the cardboard piece.
5. Trace an outline on the cardboard the same size as the open datebook, using the straight edge and pen.
6. Using the straight edge and X-acto knife, cut out the cardboard piece.
7. With the ruler, find the exact middle of the cardboard piece, mark with the pen to left and right of the center, about ¼ inch on both sides (this is at the top edge of the cardboard piece).
8. Use your straight edge to fold the cardboard piece; one fold should be where the left mark is and one should be where the right mark is. Use the bone folder to crease the folds.
9. Glue the cardboard piece to the back of the datebook by applying small dots of glue along one edge of the datebook, and press the cardboard

ECO-BIT: VINYL

You might think that you stopped buying vinyl when you made the switch to CDs, but think again. Vinyl is used in much more than your old records. You might recognize its other name, laminate. But laminate is not a material, it's a process, and just one of the ways vinyl shows up. All different types of vinyl can be recycled, but it is often used in place of more durable finishes, which may mean more waste in the long run.

down on to the cover. Keep pressure on the piece for about 20 seconds. Check to see that the glue is dry.

10. Glue the fabric to the cardboard, applying small glue dots all the way around the outer edges of the cardboard. Smooth the fabric, pulling it taut so that there are no ripples or bumps across the cover. The datebook should be placed exactly in the center of the piece of fabric—you will fold the excess fabric down on the inside of the cover. Wait for the glue to dry.

11. Cut the fabric in the center where the pages are, so that you can lay the fabric down on either side of the covers. You can use pinking shears if you'd like.

12. Cut two squares out of the wrapping paper (or whatever material you'd like to use for the inside of the cover), making sure that the squares are the exact size of the insides of the cover. Glue the pieces in place.

Note: As an extra step, add an appliqué or embroider initials for a personal touch.

STAR ORNAMENT

Vinyl and plastic are two man-made materials that truly revolutionized product design. Before that, tin was used for practically everything—from dishes to furniture to ornaments. Tin was abandoned as a go-to resources with the advent of cheaper alternatives. This star ornament harkens back to the time when tin was a popular material and there was no such thing as plastic. Because of their rarity, vintage ornaments can be costly. This star is a pretty good alternative, and it's free.

Tools and Materials

› Leather work gloves
› Tin snips
› 2 empty soda cans
› Black felt tip pen
› Star template or star-shaped cookie cutter
› Wire cutters
› Metal ruler
› Bone folder
› Newspaper
› 14-gauge utility wire
› Pencil
› Glue gun and glue sticks

How To

1. Put on leather work gloves. Use tin snips to cut the ends off of the aluminum cans and to slice them open along the seams.
2. Spread out the aluminum pieces on a flat surface.
3. Use the pen and a star template (find one online or use a cookie cutter) to draw a star pattern on the printed side of each aluminum piece.
4. Cut the stars out using the tin snips.
5. On the wrong side, set a metal ruler on the star from one star point, down the middle of the star, and to the end of the opposite point. Firmly run a bone folder along the ruler edge. Repeat until each point is scored. Lightly bend the star on each of the score lines. Repeat the process for the other star (this will make the star three dimensional).
6. Wrap wire around a pencil to form a 4-inch-long coil with 2 inches of straight wire remaining. Remove the wire from the pencil.

7. Crumple a piece of newspaper and hot glue it to the inside center of one star.
8. Place a bit of hot glue on the straight wire part of the coil and push it into the newspaper, leaving the coil sticking out of the star.
9. Glue the opposite side of the star onto the newspaper, matching the edges of both star cutouts.
10. Use the coil to attach the star to tree branches, wreaths, or anywhere you want a bit of twinkle.

SIMPLE GARLAND

Decorations may be a festive harbinger of the holiday season, but overuse of electricity is something we have to curtail. I have firsthand knowledge of the enormous energy wasted by electric lights and all that goes with them. When I was growing up, my grandparents were "those people" who basically lit up their entire house and yard with lights. Luckily, they lived on a hill surrounded by woods, with no neighbors near enough to get offended. To a little kid, this over the top display was anything but tacky. Now we know better, and make choices with less of an environmental impact. Whatever you choose to do for a little holiday style is totally up to you, so long as it doesn't upset the neighbors or drain the power grid. Look for energy-efficient light garlands—LED lights are now widely available. Or try an energy-free holiday: Skip the lights and ignite the festive spirit with this pretty holiday garland.

ECO-BIT: ENERGY DRAIN

Holiday energy use is significantly higher than at other times of the year. One of the main culprits is traditional electricity-draining lights. Switch to LED lights and you can use up to 90 percent less energy.

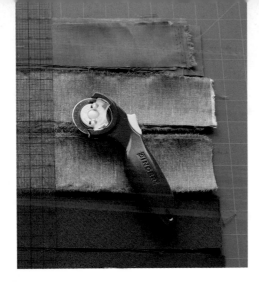

Tools and Materials

›   Fabric scissors

›   Fabric remnants from silk, organza, or velvet

›   Cutting mat

›   Clear ruler

›   Rotary cutter

›   Sewing machine

›   Thread (preferably silver, gold, or other decorative color)

How To

1. Cut fabric into strips, about 12-inches long by 2-inches wide. Use fabric such as silk or organza so that a natural fraying happens around the edges, but you can just as easily use lightweight cotton. Stack three fabric strips at a time, lining up strips that are alike if using different fabrics.

2. Cut horizontally across the stacked strips using the rotary cutter, making them into smaller squares. Cut at every 1-inch increment or vary the sizes, making some less or more than 1 inch.

3. Repeat these steps for as much fabric as you plan to use.

4. Leave a tail of thread about 10-inches long on the sewing machine. Feed each square through the machine, one at a time, stitching a visible line. Where to place the stitching on each piece isn't important, because the variety is part of the charm.

5. After stitching across each square, pull out 2 inches of thread so there's a space between it and the next fabric piece.

6. When you finish the last piece, leave a 10-inch tail of thread.

7. Tie the two ends of thread together, making a big circle that can be hung many different places, even on a tree. If you want to use this all of the time and not just for holidays, try draping it over a curtain rod, so that it hangs off each end of the rod.

Note: To store the garland so it doesn't get tangled, cut a flap off of a cardboard box, and cut a notch at the top and bottom of the flap. Place the beginning of the thread through the top notch and wind the garland around the cardboard. Secure the end of the thread in the notch at the bottom of the flap.

ECO-CHIC HOME
RESOURCE GUIDE

SUSTAINABLE STYLE

› Behind the Label, www.behindthelabel.org
› Care2 Make a Difference, www.care2.com
› Envirolink: the Online Environmental Community, www.envirolink.org
› Environmental Business Journal, www.ebiusa.com
› Environmental Defense Fund, www.edf.org
› Environmental Protection Agency, www.epa.gov
› Fair Trade Labelling Organizations International, www.fairtrade.net
› Greener Choices, www.greenerchoices.org
› Grist, www.grist.org
› Ocean Conservancy, www.oceanconservancy.org
› Treehugger, www.treehugger.com

General Recycling Information
› eBrand Aid: How to Read Product Labels, www.ebrandaid.com
› Eco-Cycle, www.ecocycle.org
› EcoMall Green Marketplace, www.ecomall.com

Interior Decorating
› Apartment Therapy, www.apartmenttherapy.com
› *The Comfort of Color, New Country Color*, and *Colorscapes: Inspiring Palettes for the Home*, all by Susan Sargent, www.susansargent.com
› Designer's Library, www.designerslibary.typepad.com
› *Downtown Chic* by Bob Novogratz and Courtney Novogratz
› *Easy Elegance: Creating a Relaxed, Comfortable and Stylish Home* by Atlanta Bartlett
› *Michael S. Smith: Elements of Style* by Michael S. Smith with Diane Dorrans Saeks
› *Old and New* by Katherine Sorrell
› Remodelista, www.remodelista.com
› Shelterrific, www.shelterrific.com

About Big-Box Stores
› Behind the Label, www.behindthelabel.org
› Fair Trade, www.fairtrade.org
› *The Walmart Effect: How the World's Most Powerful Company Really Works and How It's Transforming the American Economy* by Charles Fishman

Buying Used

› *Bazaar Style: Decorating with Market and Vintage Finds* by Selina Lake and Joanna Simmons
› Craig's List, www.craigslist.org
› eBay, www.ebay.com
› *The Find: The Housing Works Book of Decorating with Thrift Shop Treasures, Flea Market Objects, and Vintage Details* by Stan Williams, the Elegant Thrifter
› Freecycle, www.freecycle.org
› Historic House Parts, www.historichouseparts.com
› *Restoration Home* by Mark Bailey and Sally Bailey

Handmade Goods

› Artfire, www.artfire.com
› Buy Olympia, www.buyolympia.com
› *Craft Magazine,* www.craft.com
› Etsy, www.etsy.com
› Indiepublic, www.indiepublic.com
› Modern Economy Home and Lifestyle Sample Sale, www.modeconomy.com
› Olio United, www.oliounited.com
› Original Good, www.originalgood.com
› Tipnut, www.tipnut.com

Thrifting

› Goodwill Industries, www.goodwill.org
› Holly Lane Antiques, www.antiquearts.com
› Housing Works, www.housingworksauctions.com
› Mennonite Thrift Shop Network, www.mcc.org
› Savers Stores, www.savers.com
› The Thrift Shopper, www.thethriftshopper.com
› Thrifttown Thrift Stores, www.thrifttown.com

Flea Markets

› National Flea Market Association, www.fleamarkets.org
› Greenflea Inc., www.greenfleamarkets.com
› *The Flea Markets of France* by Sandy Price
› *Paris: Made by Hand* by Pia Jane Bijkerk

Thrifting Online

› Collectors, www.collectors.com

Famous Fleas: The Antiques Garage NYC, www.hellskitchenfleamarket.com; The Brimfield Antiques Show, www.brimfield.com; The Brooklyn Flea, www.brownstowner.com/brooklynflea; the Paris Flea Market (Le Puces De Paris Saint-Ouen), www.parispuces.com; Portobello Market, www.portobellomarket.org; Covent Garden Market, www.coventgardenlondonuk.com

Emily's Favorites: The Elephant's Trunk Country Flea Market, www.etflea.com (Connecticut); Kane County Flea Market Show, www.kanecountyfleamarket.com (Chicago); Round Top Antiques Fair, www.roundtoptexas.com (Austin area); Scott Antique Market, www.scottantiquemarket.com (Atlanta); Todd Farm Antiques and Flea Market, www.toddfarm.com (Boston)

> The Freecycle Network, www.Freecycle.org
> Goodwill Too!, www.goodwilltoo.com

Salvaging Materials
> 2Good2Toss, www.2good2toss.com
> Building Materials Resource Center, www.bostonbmrc.org/bostonbmrc/index.html
> Building Materials Reuse Association, www.bmra.org
> Building Resources, www.buildingresources.org
> Deconstruction Institute, www.deconstructioninstitute.com
> The Green Project, www.thegreenproject.org
> Habitat for Humanity ReStores, www.habitat.org
> Rejuvenation classic lighting and house parts, www.rejuvenation.com
> Renovators Resource, www.renovators-resource.com
> *The Resourceful Renovator: A Gallery of Ideas for Reusing Building Materials* by Jennifer Carson
> Scrap House, www.scraphouse.org

Tools and More
> AC Moore, www.acmoore.com
> Dick Blick, www.dickblick.com.
> *Field Guide to Tools* by John Kelsey (*This Old House* magazine)
> Garber Hardware, www.garberhardware.com
> Maker SHED DIY Kits + Tools + Books + Fun, www.makershed.com
> McGuckin Hardware, www.mcguckin.com
> Tool Shopping Guide, www.toolshoppingguide.com
> Van Dyke's Restorers, www.vandykes.com
> Woodworks Ltd., www.craftparts.com
> Woodcraft Supply, www.woodcraft.com

Paint and More
> Allerdice Building Supply, www.allerdice.com
> Artist and Craftsman Supply, www.artistcraftsman.com
> Bioshield Healthy Living Paints, www.bioshieldpaint.com
> Brooklyn General Store, www.brooklyngeneral.com
> Dharma Trading Fiber Art Supplies, www.dharmatrading.com
> Mod Green Pod, www.modgreenpod.com
> Mythic nontoxic paint, www.mythicpaint.com
> The Genuine Old-Fashioned Milk Paint Co., www.milkpaint.com
> Olympic low-VOC paint, www.olympic.com
> Paperworks, www.paperworks.com

Fabric and Sewing Supplies
> Brooklyn General Store, www.brooklyngeneral.com
> Calico Corners, www.calicocorners.com
> *Complete Photo Guide to Sewing* by the Editors of *Creative Publishing*

- › Fabric.com, www.fabric.com
- › JoAnn fabric and craft stores, www.joann.com
- › Purl Patchwork, www.purlsoho.com
- › *Readers Digest: New Complete Guide to Sewing* by the Editors of *Readers Digest*
- › Sew Fast Sew Easy, www.sewfastseweasy.com
- › Sew Mama Sew, www.sewmamasew.com
- › Singer Co., www.singerco.com

ENTRYWAY

Clutter Solutions
- › Clothespins: eBay, www.ebay.com
- › The Vermont Country Store, www.thevermontcountrystore.com

Take Your Name Off Mailing Lists
- › MailStopper (formerly Greendimes), www.mailstopper.tonic.com
- › Direct Marketing Association, www.dmachoice.org
- › ProQuo, www.proquo.com
- › Do Not Mail petition, www.donotmail.org

Grandfather Clock
- › Used wall clocks: Planet Office Furniture, www.planetofficefurniture.com

LIVING ROOM

Reupholstered Chair
- › Ornamental rounds and trim: Horton Brasses, www.horton-brasses.com

Keepsake Album
- › Ribbons and buttons: Caramelos Artful Supplies, www.caramelos.etsy.com

Floor Cushions
- › Textile fabric: Trans World Sourcing, www.twstrading.com

File Drawer Side Table
- › Cube King: Office Furniture Discounters, www.cubeking.com

KITCHEN

Countertop Resources
- › Duro Design, www.durodesign.com
- › Eco-Flex recycled rubber tires, www.eco-flex.com
- › Enviroglas recycled glass, www.enviroglasproducts.com

> VitraStone recycled glass, www.vitrastone.com

Door Do-Over
> Decorative molding and appliqué pieces: Dyke's Lumber Company, www.dykeslumber.com

Trays
> Used baking supplies: Apple Restaurant Supply, www.applerestaurantsupply.com

Understanding Product Labels
> *Consumer Reports* GreenerChoices Eco-labels Center, www.greenerchoices.org/eco-labels/eco-home.cfm

Old Door Knobs and Handles
> The Old House Parts Company, www.oldhouseparts.com.

Spice Rack
> Used shelf brackets: Rejuvenation, www.rejuvenation.com

Storage Ideas
> Used kitchen stuff: A City Discount, www.acitydiscount.com

DINING ROOM

Remade Dishware
> Stencils: Designer Stencils, www.designerstencils.com
> Small butane torch: Metal Clay Supply Store, www.metalclaysupplystore.com

Tablescapes
> Jamie Oliver, www.jamieoliver.com
> *Table Inspirations: Original Ideas, Stylish Entertaining* by Emily Chalmers

Mismatched China Pieces
> Dish Factory, www.dishfactory.com

Independent Tableware Producers
> Terra Keramik, www.terrakeramik.com

Chair Cover
> Used linen fabric: Primrose Design, www.primrosedesign.com

Extra Table
> Oilcloth fabric remnants: Mendel's Far Out Fabrics, www.mendels.com

Natural Centerpiece
> Cherry blossom stencil: Stencil Library, www.stencil-library.com

BEDROOM

Braided Rug
› Used cotton T-shirts: Green Village Used Clothing by the Pound, Brooklyn, New York, www.gogreenvillage.com. Not in Brooklyn? Search online for similar stores in your area.

Ladder Clothes Rack
› Used ladders: Storage Solutions, www.storage-solutions.com

Folding Screen
› Used shutters: The Antique Wood Co., www.antiquewoodco.com
› Craig's List, www.craigslist.com
› eBay, www.ebay.com
› Freecycle, www.freecycle.org

Better Bleach and Other Cleaning Supplies
› Green Works, www.greenworkscleaners.com
› Method products, www.methodhome.com

Dry Cleaning Facts
› Sierra Club, *The Dirty Facts About Dry Cleaning*, www.sierraclub.org/cleanair/drycleaners/factsheet.pdf

Mothballs and Alternatives
› Dried lavender: Lavender Green, www.lavendergreen.com

LIGHTING

› Bom Design Studio, www.bomdesign.nl
› Light bulb sources: Choose Renewables, www.chooserenewables.com

Handmade Vase Lamp
› Used vases: Ruby Lane, www.rubylane.com.
› Lamp parts: The Lamp Shop, www.lampshop.com
› Electrical wiring: *Ultimate Guide to Wiring: Complete Projects for the Home* (paperback) by the Editors of *Creative Homeowner*

Clip-On Lamp
› Master Hole Saw Kit: Dewalt D180005 14 Piece Master Hole Saw Kit, www.dewalt.com
› Lamp kit: Sunshine Crafts, www.sunshinecrafts.com
› Ecobond, www. ecobond.com

Bookshelf Lamp
› Used CDs: Amazon, www.amazon.com
› Lamp parts: The Lamp Shop, www.lampshop.com

Vintage Factory Lighting
› Olde Good Things, www.ogtstore.com

Light Garland
› LED light strand: Choose Renewables, www.chooserenewables.com

Candlestick Display
› Used candlesticks: Ruby Lane, www.rubylane.com
› Glitter: Art Institute Glitter, www.artglitter.com

Tea Cup Candles
› Candles and candlemaking supplies: Betterbee, www.betterbee.com

Covered Matchbooks
› Matches: Atlas Match, www.atlasmatch.com
› Get Matches, www.getmatches.com
› Pretty papers: D. Blumchen and Company, www.blumchen.com

HOLIDAYS AND GIFT GIVING

Mindful Celebrations
› *Last Minute Patchwork and Quilted Gifts* by Joelle Hoverson (at purlsoho.com)
› *Paperie for Inspired Living: Stationery and Decorations for Weddings, Parties, and Other Special Occasions* by Karen Bartolomei
› Use Less Stuff, www.use-less-stuff.com
› Balloons: Eco My Party, www.ecomyparty.com
› More papier mâché: Ultimate Papier Mâché, www.ultimatepapiermache.com

Creative Gift Wrap
› WrapArt by John Boak, www.boakart.com/wrap/wrapart.html

Christmas Trees
› About forest stewardship: American Tree Farm System, www.treefarmsystem.org
› Cut your own: Christmas Tree Farm Network, www.christmas-tree.com
› Recycling your tree: Earth911, www.earth911.com

Star Ornament
› Star-shaped cookie cutters: Aunt Holly Cookie Cutters, www.aunthollycookiecutters.com
› Star template: Jan Dressler Stencils, www.dresslerstencils.com

Simple Garland
› Fabric remnants: Etsy, www.etsy.com
› Purl and Purl Patchwork, www.purlsoho.com

ACKNOWLEDGMENTS

My biggest thanks go to my husband David. I am grateful everyday for you and feel so blessed to have you in my life.

I also give my gratitude to photographers Kendra and Seth Smoot. Your integrity and the beauty of your work are incredible and rare. I could not have asked for better partners in this insanely labor-intensive project! Anne Gorfinkle opened up her beautiful home to us in the most generous, supportive way. It was the perfect environment to showcase our projects, and the images in this book would not be what they are without you.

Dana Youlin, my editor at Skipstone: Thank you for believing in this project and for understanding the challenges I had to deal with along the way. I know it hasn't been easy! I am also very fortunate to have such a strong supporter in Kate Rogers, Editor in Chief at Skipstone, who believed that I could write something great. I appreciate your calm and steady support. Meghan Meyers was generous enough to put me in touch with Skipstone in the first place. I am so grateful to have you as my friend and kindred spirit in this crazy space. You are the real deal, and we both know how rare and precious that is.

To my big brother Jamie, thanks for always looking out for me and for taking on more than your share of the burden so I had the time to finish this project. Thank you Alexis Anthony for bringing your skill and style to the table literally at the very last minute—you helped get us to the finish line. Darcy Miller, I am so honored that you have supported me during and after my time at Martha Stewart. You are a wonderful person and *Martha Stewart Weddings* would not be what it is without you. I also want to say thank you to Martha Stewart herself: You created a company that champions the crafter, the creator, and the individual entrepreneur. Without you I would not have had the opportunity to follow my own dreams.

My children are too small to read this but someday they will, and I need them to know how important they both were in this process. Sam, you were just born when I had to turn so much of my attention to getting this book completed, and your little smiling face gave me the encouragement I needed. Sydney Lulu you are my little treasure; thank you for being Mommy's assistant, and I can't wait until you are old enough to use my tools—I can see the sparkle of a crafter in your eyes already.

Thanks to my father and Margaret for supporting and encouraging me. I love you both very much. As always I need to remember my mother; I wish I could have seen you in action—building, baking, and crafting your little world into the warm wonderful place it was. Thank you to my mother-in-law Cecille Natt for your patience, support, and understanding when I couldn't come to visit because I was working. And Cece—thank you in advance for the PR I know you will get for me at the Radnor Curves. You rock! I also am very grateful to HP.

Finally, I have eternal gratitude to my grandmothers, Marion and Lucille, who are both gone now but their energy, style, and love continues to inspire me everyday. You were incredible women, and I hope I make you proud.

INDEX